Comprehensive Fundraising Campaigns

Comprehensive Fundraising Campaigns

New Directions for Colleges and Universities

Michael J. Worth

ROWMAN & LITTLEFIELD
Lanham • Boulder • New York • London

Published by Rowman & Littlefield
An imprint of The Rowman & Littlefield Publishing Group, Inc.
4501 Forbes Boulevard, Suite 200, Lanham, Maryland 20706
www.rowman.com

86-90 Paul Street, London EC2A 4NE, United Kingdom

Copyright © 2022 by Michael J. Worth

All rights reserved. No part of this book may be reproduced in any form or by any electronic or mechanical means, including information storage and retrieval systems, without written permission from the publisher, except by a reviewer who may quote passages in a review.

British Library Cataloguing in Publication Information Available

Library of Congress Cataloging-in-Publication Data Available

Names: Worth, Michael J., author.
Title: Comprehensive fundraising campaigns : new directions for colleges and universities / Michael J. Worth.
Description: Lanham, Maryland : Rowman & Littlefield, [2022] | Includes bibliographical references. | Summary: "This book provides a review of comprehensive campaigns in higher education and their role in institutional strategy and growth"— Provided by publisher.
Identifiers: LCCN 2021047737 (print) | LCCN 2021047738 (ebook) | ISBN 9781475862126 (Cloth) | ISBN 9781475862133 (Paperback) | ISBN 9781475862140 (ePub)
Subjects: LCSH: Educational fund raising—United States—Evaluation. | Education, Higher—United States—Finance. | Universities and colleges—United States—Endowments. | Benefactors—Charitable contributions—United States. | Strategic planning—United States.
Classification: LCC LB2336 .W666 2022 (print) | LCC LB2336 (ebook) | DDC 378.1/06—dc23/eng/20211103
LC record available at https://lccn.loc.gov/2021047737
LC ebook record available at https://lccn.loc.gov/2021047738

Contents

Acknowledgments	vii
Introduction	ix
Chapter 1: The Comprehensive Campaign	1
PART I: DOCTORAL UNIVERSITIES	25
Chapter 2: Rochester Institute of Technology	29
Chapter 3: Tulane University	41
Chapter 4: University of Virginia	53
PART II: MASTER'S COLLEGES AND UNIVERSITIES	65
Chapter 5: California State University, Los Angeles	67
Chapter 6: Youngstown State University	79
PART III: BACCALAUREATE COLLEGES	91
Chapter 7: St. John's College	95
Chapter 8: Spelman College	105
PART IV: ASSOCIATE'S COLLEGES	117
Chapter 9: Central Piedmont Community College	121
Chapter 10: New Directions: The Years Ahead	133
Further Reading	147
About the Author	149

Acknowledgments

The author expresses gratitude to the following individuals, who offered helpful suggestions on this project: Karin L. George, Managing Principal, Washburn & McGoldrick; John J. Glier, Chief Executive Officer, Grenzebach Glier and Associates (GG+A); Philippe G. Hills, President & CEO, Marts & Lundy; Richard D. Legon, Immediate Past President and Senior Consultant, Association of Governing Boards of Universities and Colleges; and Marc Westenburg, Director of the Center for Community College Advancement, Council for Advancement and Support of Education.

The case studies in this book are based in part on interviews with chief advancement officers and, in some cases, other advancement professionals at the institutions. The author expresses gratitude to the following individuals for their participation:

Jessie L. Brooks, Vice President for Advancement, Spelman College (Interviewed June 1, 2021);

Kelly Brown, Vice President of Advancement, Campaign Director, St. John's College (Interviewed April 20, 2021);

Phillip D. Castleberry, Vice President for University Advancement, Rochester Institute of Technology (Interviewed February 25, 2021);

Janet Schellhase Dial, Vice President for University Advancement, Cal State LA, and Executive Director of the Cal State LA Foundation (Interviewed June 7, 2021);

Christine Hoffman, Vice President, Campaigns and Administration, Tulane University (Interviewed April 26, 2021, May 11, 2021);

Mark M. Luellen, Vice President for Advancement, University of Virginia (Interviewed January 28, 2021);

Kevin McCarthy, Executive Vice President for Institutional Advancement, Central Piedmont Community College (Interviewed June 22, 2021);

Paul J. McFadden, President, Youngstown State University Foundation (Interviewed March 18, 2021);

Eileen Galinski Thrall, Assistant Vice President for University Advancement, Principal Gifts and University Campaigns, Rochester Institute of Technology (Interviewed February 17, 2021);

Ginny Wise, Senior Vice President for Advancement, Tulane University (Interviewed May 11, 2021)

Introduction

Organized fundraising campaigns have been a part of American higher education since the early years of the twentieth century and have become a visible and highly important activity of colleges and universities. Today, most institutions are either conducting or planning a campaign, with only a brief—if any—gap between such initiatives.

Campaigns have evolved over the decades. What were once known as capital campaigns have become comprehensive campaigns, umbrellas over all fundraising of the college or university and often also including goals for marketing, communications, branding, and engagement. Comprehensive campaigns are a common strategy for advancing institutions in the United States and, increasingly, in other nations as well.

Institutions continue to pursue new campaign strategies in order to adapt to changing external conditions and institutional priorities. As Fritz Schroeder (2019, p. 126), vice president for development and alumni relations at the Johns Hopkins University, explains, "Many of the campaign principles established over a century ago are still relevant. But it will be essential to adapt the historic model to reflect the new forces affecting higher education today and in the future."

The purpose of the case studies assembled in this book is not to establish campaign "best practices" or to highlight the most "successful" campaigns as measured by high dollar goals. Although many conventional best practices are evident in the campaigns that are discussed, some also demonstrate unique approaches.

In each of the cases in the following chapters of this book, a comprehensive campaign was a central part of an institutional strategy for growth and change. Many of the campaigns marked a turning point in the institution's history—a transition to a new presidency, recovery from a disaster, a redefinition of the mission, adoption of a new strategic plan or funding model, and other critical events. For that reason, the case studies do not focus totally on fundraising. They start with an overview of the university's history, traditions, leadership, programs, and institutional strategies, which establish the context for the campaign. *These are not just stories about campaigns, they are stories about institutions and their strategies for growth and change.*

Some academic works related to campaigns are cited in appropriate places in this book, but it also draws on the abundant practitioner literature. It is intended to be of interest to institutional leaders involved in planning and managing comprehensive campaigns, as well as to board members and others who play some leadership role in campaigns. It may also be of interest to scholars who seek to add to the body of research specifically focused on campaigns. That literature is currently limited, although there is a larger literature addressing the broader topics of fundraising and philanthropy.

The case studies presented in the following chapters were based on an initial outline and protocol for interviews. Indeed, those materials were reviewed and approved by the appropriate research office of the George Washington University, where the author is a professor. However, the studies evolved in various directions and the chapters are organized somewhat differently, reflecting the unique circumstances of the institutions and campaigns that were explored.

There are various published lists of campaigns, which served as a starting point in selecting the institutions for the studies. The Council for Advancement and Support of Education (CASE) provides a list of the largest campaigns and the publication Inside Higher Ed maintains a list of campaigns that is updated periodically. The author used the Inside Higher Ed list, since it includes a range of campaign goals and not just the largest.

Institutions were selected to include various types, based on the Carnegie Classification of Institutions of Higher Education, both public and private and in various geographic regions. The Carnegie Classifications were created by the Carnegie Commission on Higher Education in 1970 and were updated periodically by the Carnegie Foundation until 2014, when the responsibility was transferred to the Center for Postsecondary Research of the Indiana University School of Education in Bloomington, Indiana (Carnegie Classification of Institutions of Higher Education, n.d.). The classifications used in this book were those published in 2019. A 2021 revision of the classifications was expected to be published late that year and finalized in early 2022, after the deadline for completion of this book. No major changes were anticipated (Borden, 2021).

The list was narrowed to campaigns that were underway when this project began in 2020, so that public documents would be readily available and, given the common reality of staff turnover at the conclusion of a campaign, so that interviews could be obtained with institutional officers who had been directly involved.

Once the list had been narrowed as discussed above, the author reviewed websites and news articles to identify institutions and campaigns that might provide "interesting stories," obviously a subjective judgment. The author also consulted with three prominent fundraising consultants and an official of the Council for Advancement and Support of Education to obtain suggestions of campaigns that might demonstrate unique features. All case studies were submitted for review by the institution's chief advancement officer as a draft, to assure accuracy. Those individuals provided useful corrections and clarifications. Any remaining errors are those of the author.

IN A TIME OF TURMOIL AND CHANGE

It is important to note that the case studies included in this book were conducted over a period of months in 2020 and 2021, beginning during a particularly serious phase of the Covid-19 pandemic. Obviously, university fundraising, like all human activities, was significantly impacted by that public health crisis. While the effects of the pandemic are a part of the story in the campaigns studied, that is not a primary focus of this work.

Many observers predicted that the post-Covid world would not be the same as it was before. However, to a considerable extent, the pandemic may have accelerated changes that already were underway. The case studies acknowledge the impact of the pandemic but also take a broader perspective. They reflect a number of trends and patterns that were already affecting campaigns before the pandemic's onset and that are likely to remain relevant after it has subsided.

It is important to clarify, again, that the studies were completed over a period of months. The campaigns studied were in various stages at the time that the author turned his attention to them. Each study includes information available up to the point of submission of the book manuscript to the publisher. For those campaigns that were still ongoing at that point, there may be more to the story that the case study does not capture. Readers may wish to do their own research on the Web to obtain more recent information.

OVERVIEW OF CHAPTERS

Chapter 1 provides a history and overview of comprehensive campaigns. It draws in part on the author's previous work, including two editions of *Leading the Campaign*, which explored the art and science of campaign planning and management in some detail (Worth, 2010, 2017). This chapter may be of particular interest to those who are relatively new to the topic.

The following chapters are divided into four parts, each including cases from institutions in one of the Carnegie categories. Part I includes three cases from Doctoral Universities (the Rochester Institute of Technology, Tulane University, and the University of Virginia). Part II contains two cases from Master's Colleges and Universities (California State University, Los Angeles and Youngstown State University). Part III presents cases based on two Liberal Arts Colleges (St. John's College and Spelman College). Part IV includes one case from an Associate's College (Central Piedmont Community College). This selection does not cover all of the sub-classifications utilized by the Carnegie framework or some other institution types, such as specialized institutions or tribal colleges. But these classifications encompass most of the higher education institutions in the United States. The final chapter reflects on the case studies, identifies some common themes, and discusses possible new directions for colleges and universities in future comprehensive campaigns.

Colleges and universities are among the most important institutions in our society. They create new knowledge, prepare future generations for leadership, and model ideals that are essential to a free and democratic society. Advancing such institutions is vitally important work. It is hoped that this book may provide some insights that will be useful to colleges and universities in securing the resources essential to advancement of their missions—and that readers may find it to be interesting.

REFERENCES

Borden, Victor M. H. 2021. (Professor of Higher Education and Student Affairs, Project Director, Carnegie Classification of Institutions of Higher Education, Indiana University School of Education). Email to author, May 19, 2021.

Carnegie Classification of Institutions of Higher Education. n.d. http://carnegieclassifications.iu.edu/ (accessed May 3, 2021).

Schroder, Fritz W. 2019. "The Art and Science of Comprehensive Campaigns." In *Advancing Higher Education: New Strategies for Fundraising, Philanthropy, and Engagement*, edited by Michael J. Worth and Matthew T. Lambert, 113–128. Lanham, MD: Rowman & Littlefield.

Worth, Michael J. 2010. *Leading the Campaign: Advancing Colleges and Universities*. Lanham, MD: Rowman & Littlefield and American Council on Higher Education.

Worth, Michael J. 2017. *Leading the Campaign: The President and Fundraising in Higher Education*. Lanham, MD: Rowman & Littlefield.

Chapter 1

The Comprehensive Campaign

In 1641, William Hibbens, Hugh Peter, and Thomas Weld set sail from America to London on a mission to raise funds for a struggling young educational institution in Massachusetts. Bearing what may have been the first example of fundraising literature, a brochure entitled "New England's First Fruits," this team solicited support for the purpose of "educating the heathen Indian," a cause that was deemed worthy by wealthy British citizens of the time. Their efforts were met with mixed results. As historian Scott Cutlip reports, Weld remained in England and never returned to America. So, too, in a way, did Peter, who was hanged there for crimes he committed under British law. Only Hibbens returned to Massachusetts, a year later, with £500 for Harvard College. As Cutlip dryly observes, "Such were the rewards of early fund raisers" (Cutlip, 1965, p. 4).

Today's higher education leaders might say that raising funds for a college or university is still a daunting challenge. But, while it remains a combination of art and science, fundraising has become considerably more systematic since the early adventures of Hibbens, Peter, and Weld. College and university fundraising initiatives are well planned, highly organized, and tightly managed, including the campaigns that are the focus of this book.

FROM BEGGING TO STRATEGY

Many people still refer to any college or university campaign as a "capital campaign." It is a term familiar to many people. Capital projects and endowment (financial capital) are among the objectives of many campaigns, so it is not entirely inaccurate. But most campaigns in higher education today are *comprehensive campaigns*, encompassing capital projects, endowment, annual giving, and support restricted to specific current programs and research. Most comprehensive campaigns encompass all gifts and commitments for all purposes over a defined period of years—they are umbrellas over all fundraising efforts of the institution. How we got to this model—the history of campaigns in higher education—is an interesting story that is worth understanding. It demonstrates how the concept of a campaign has adapted—and continues to evolve—in response to significant changes in higher education, patterns of wealth, tax law, the economy, and society.

In the nation's early centuries, fundraising for higher education was primitive by today's standards. It consisted mostly of "passing the church plate, of staging church suppers or bazaars, and writing 'begging letters'" (Cutlip, 1965, p. 7). Indeed, since many early colleges were related to a sponsoring church, their presidents were often clergy and appeals for funds often reflected a religious tone. In that period, the case for support of American colleges often was based on the desire to advance Christianity and prepare young men for the ministry (Cutlip, 1965, p. 3).

In the years before the twentieth century, fundraising was primarily a personal transaction between asker and giver and involved far more art than science. The revolution in fundraising came in the first decade of the twentieth century, and it began outside of higher education.

THE HISTORICAL CAPITAL CAMPAIGN

In 1902, YMCA executive Lyman L. Pierce launched a campaign to raise $300,000 toward construction of a new building in Washington, DC. By 1905, he had come within $80,000 of that goal, but the effort had stalled. Pierce called for help from another YMCA executive who had built a reputation as a successful fundraiser, Charles Sumner Ward from Chicago. Ward came to Washington to help rejuvenate the campaign, which he successfully completed. As Cutlip (1965, p. 44) describes, "The collaboration of Ward and Pierce produced the first modern fundraising campaign techniques: careful organization, picked leadership spurred on by team competition, prestige leaders, powerful publicity, a large gift to be matched, careful records, report meetings, and a definite time limit."

The process that Ward introduced subsequently became known as the Ward method and encompassed many of the techniques that characterize a campaign today, with modifications and refinements developed by many other practitioners since. Ward's contribution was not only the introduction of specific fundraising practices, but also the very idea that adherence to a system and skill in management are more important than personal charisma in defining a successful fundraiser (Cutlip, 1965, p. 9). Ward's approach to fundraising was focused on management of the process and the application of insights about human psychology and sociology, rather than the begging that had characterized such efforts in earlier times.

Following his success with the YMCA, Ward was retained by the University of Pittsburgh to manage a campaign for $3 million, bringing his method into higher education. Some of the people whom Ward hired to work with him in Pittsburgh subsequently founded their own consulting firms that extended Ward's approach to college and university campaigns across the country in the following decades.

Indeed, until about the mid-1960s, most campaigns were directed by consultants from such firms, who would take up residence on campus for a period of months to guide the president and volunteers through the intensive portion of the campaign, and then move on to a new assignment elsewhere. It was a model, and a lifestyle, that gave rise to some influential and colorful personalities of organized fundraising's early days.

Beginning in about the mid-1960s—and at an accelerating pace over following decades—colleges and universities appointed full-time development officers to manage ongoing fundraising programs and campaigns, reducing the need for the resident-manager model of consulting. Today even small colleges have a development or advancement staff of at least several people, and large research universities employ hundreds of professionals, led by a vice president who is a seasoned campaign manager. Consultants continue to play a role in campaign planning and often provide ongoing campaign advice.

The term advancement was introduced with the founding of the Council for Advancement and Support of Education (CASE) in 1974 and encompasses the professional fields of fundraising (development), marketing and communications, and alumni relations or engagement. Many vice presidents are their institution's "chief advancement officer" and some have responsibility for all of those programs. Other institutions separate the responsibilities and have vice presidents with titles that include "development and alumni relations," "communications and marketing," or something similar.

Nevertheless, it is generally agreed that there needs to be close coordination among the various advancement programs regardless of reporting responsibilities and, indeed, that is especially important in the context of a campaign.

FROM CAPITAL TO COMPREHENSIVE

Before the 1970s, most college and university campaigns were capital campaigns, or, as Kent Dove calls them in his classic book, "historical" capital campaigns, since the model is essentially obsolete in higher education now (Dove, 2000, p. 16). However, it should be noted that nonprofit organizations and institutions outside of education still often conduct capital campaigns. Like the campaigns that Ward and his contemporaries directed, capital campaigns were special, intensive efforts, conducted about once or twice a decade, usually to raise funds for construction of a new campus building. The campaign generally consumed all of the institution's fundraising energies for a period of time (usually about three years) and included solicitation of its *entire constituency* for one-time commitments toward the featured project.

Alumni annual giving funds were created in the nineteenth century and many had become ongoing programs by early in the twentieth. But the annual fund was often suspended for the duration of a capital campaign or was continued as a separate, low-key effort. All attention was focused on the campaign as the institution's highest priority, and all donors were asked to support it as theirs. Of course, there were a number of shortcomings to this model.

First, donors might simply redirect their usual annual gift to the campaign, accomplishing little but to transfer money from one of the institution's pockets to another. The second problem was how to assure that individuals who had made multiyear pledges to the capital campaign would resume annual giving once their campaign pledges were completed. Restarting or rejuvenating the annual fund was often a significant challenge. And by suspending annual giving for the period of the campaign, the institution was not building its pipeline of younger donors who might become prospects for major gifts in a future campaign. The solution that emerged was to incorporate annual giving in the overall campaign and encourage donors to combine a capital gift and their annual giving into a single multiyear commitment.

Then things became even more complicated. The 1970s brought a new environment for what we now call planned giving. Some forms of planned giving, for example, bequests and gift annuities, appeared quite early in history and had always been among the largest sources of endowment gifts. But promotion of this type of giving by colleges and universities was fairly casual prior to passage of the Tax Reform Act of 1969.

The 1969 legislation defined an array of giving vehicles, including charitable remainder trusts, charitable lead trusts, and pooled income funds. Along with various pieces of legislation enacted in the years since, it still defines the ballpark for planned giving. Its passage opened up a new era in higher education fundraising that has seen increased marketing of planned giving by colleges and universities. Beginning in about the 1970s, colleges and universities expanded the definition of the campaign to integrate capital, annual, and planned gifts under one umbrella—the *comprehensive campaign*. The trend toward this approach accelerated in subsequent decades.

Like the historical capital campaign, a comprehensive campaign seeks support from the entire constituency of the institution. But rather than focusing the entire constituency on a single capital project or purpose, the campaign emphasizes various priorities across the institution. The market is differentiated, in other words, donors are solicited for support of specific campaign priorities coinciding with their interests and capabilities. Various types of commitments are credited toward the campaign goal, according to a campaign counting policy that the institution has defined. Most comprehensive campaigns count all gifts to all purposes over the period of the campaign.

By the twenty-first century, comprehensive campaigns had become the norm in higher education. A survey by the Council for Advancement and Support of Education in 2013 found that 91 percent of responding institutions intended to use some campaign funds for capital projects, 80 percent intended to use campaign gifts for endowment, and 73 percent were planning to use campaign proceeds to support current operations (CASE, 2013, p. 26).

A Broadening Definition of What Counts

The growing complexity of gifts that are encompassed in a campaign has driven the development of guidelines for how various revenues should be counted toward the campaign goal, with the purpose of achieving transparency and enabling institutional leaders to make realistic comparisons with campaigns at other institutions. The topic has sometimes led to debates. The Council for Advancement and Support of Education (CASE) developed its first set of campaign reporting standards in 1982 and has revised them periodically, resulting in the most recent CASE Global Reporting Standards, published in 2021 (CASE, 2021). A full discussion of provisions in the 2021 CASE guidelines is beyond the scope of this chapter, but a few points illustrate how complicated campaign accounting has become.

One significant recommendation in the CASE standards is that campaign totals exclude gifts received before the defined campaign period, often called "reach-back gifts." Although the guidelines acknowledge that some universities do count such gifts, and sometimes add them to campaign totals post-hoc, the practice is strongly discouraged (CASE, 2021).

CASE recommends reporting campaign commitments in three categories, in order to clarify that gifts may impact the institution on differing time frames: 1) total outright gifts and pledges received, 2) total irrevocable deferred gifts received, and 3) total revocable deferred gifts received. The standards suggest that revocable gift commitments, for example, bequest provisions, be counted toward the campaign only if the donor is age 65 at the end of the year or campaign. And the standards do not anticipate the counting of government funds in campaign totals (CASE, 2021).

One challenge in managing comprehensive campaigns is maintaining clear communication and transparency about campaign totals across the institution and among its various constituencies. Failure to do so can lead to misunderstanding and planning based on erroneous assumptions. Annual gifts are available to support current operating budgets during the campaign and gifts for research and specific programs will have been expended over the course of the campaign for those purposes. Funds given to support capital projects may be available for those purposes within a relatively brief period of years and the construction provides tangible evidence of the campaign's impact. But the impact of planned bequests will be realized only at some—unpredictable—future time when the donors pass away.

It is important that everyone understands that the end of a comprehensive campaign and achievement of its goal does not imply a pot of money that is available for allocation across the campus. Some will already have been spent and some will arrive only in years ahead. The CASE standards can help to reinforce that reality.

The CASE standards are recommended best practices and not law. They also differ in significant ways from the Generally Accepted Accounting Principles (GAAP) that apply to institutional financial statements, for example, in the crediting of pledges. But they do define the rules by which institutions report their philanthropic and campaign totals to CASE and provide a basis for comparison among institutions.

Some institutions have adopted campaign counting rules that are more expansive than the CASE guidelines recommend, reflecting their particular institutional and campaign strategies (Joslyn, 2019a). Recognizing that reality, Eynon and Hastings (2021) emphasize the importance of *transparency*, writing that "When there is a need for your campaign counting guidelines to differ from the CASE standards, it is important for your institution to be transparent and report that difference in an appropriate way so it is apparent to board members, as well as internal and external audiences, when reviewing your campaign reports" (p. 114).

Longer Campaigns, Higher Goals

In addition to a more expansive definition of what gifts are included, the length of campaigns also has increased over the decades. The historical capital campaign included about one to three years of active solicitation, with perhaps a three-to-five-year period allowed for the fulfillment of pledges. Since most campaigns were focused on a single building project, the payment of pledges in a relatively short time period was essential. Since the time at which the institution would receive control of a planned gift was unpredictable, such gifts were obviously not useful in support of such a project.

By the twenty-first century most comprehensive campaigns were continuing much longer, thus encompassing more annual giving and providing more time for the identification, cultivation, and solicitation of prospects for principal and major gifts to meet capital and endowment goals. CASE's 2021 standards suggest that campaigns not exceed eight years, but provide for flexibility and acknowledge that some run even for a decade or even longer (CASE, 2021).

In 2018, Columbia University announced a campaign with a goal of $5 billion that was planned to run for just five years (Xia, 2018). Some observers wondered if that would establish an example that would lead to shorter campaigns, noting that more extended campaigns do face challenges in maintaining urgency and focus (Schroeder, 2019, p. 125). In addition, Fritz Schroeder (2019, p. 125), vice president for development and alumni relations at Johns Hopkins, speculated that briefer presidential tenures, averaging under seven years in 2016, also might contribute to a trend toward shorter campaigns in the future.

However, working against shorter campaigns is the reality that many institutions desire to have the goal of any new campaign be larger than the previous campaign and at least as large as that of other institutions that they view as peers or competitors. In that view, a large campaign may enhance the institution's image and brand and provide opportunities to bring new donors into the pipeline.

Campaign dollar goals have increased dramatically over the decades. As an example, Harvard's campaign in 1904–1905 raised $2.5 million for faculty salaries. Its next campaign, in 1919–1920 raised $14 million for the Harvard endowment. By the late 1950s, Harvard raised what historian Scott Cutlip (1965, p. 480) calls "the staggering sum of $82,775,553." Cutlip surely would have been staggered again when, in 2018, Harvard set a new record, closing its most recent campaign with a total of $9.6 billion in commitments (Guillaume and Halper, 2018).

While campaigns were once a strategy pursued primarily by independent colleges and universities, campaigns also have become the norm at public institutions, which have set and achieved impressive goals. For example, in 2020, the University of California Berkeley launched a comprehensive campaign with a goal of $6 billion, claimed to be the largest in history for a public university without a medical school (Kell, 2020). Community Colleges, historically reliant on tuition and government funding, also have expanded their fundraising and some have initiated comprehensive campaigns; one is included as a case study in this book.

CAMPAIGN DEFINING CHARACTERISTICS

Exactly what is a "campaign" and how does it differ from just "fundraising"? While campaigns have evolved over the decades—and continue to do so—they have some long-established defining characteristics. Some remain from Ward's original method that was discussed previously and others reflect adaptation of the model to meet changing purposes and circumstances.

As the case studies in this book illustrate, campaigns at some institutions in recent years have departed from the defining characteristics discussed in this section, although most still reflect most of them in some form. And it is important to emphasize that some observers propose alternatives to the traditional campaign model. Some of those views are considered in the concluding chapter of this book.

Announced Goal and Deadline

As we have seen many times in crises and disasters, people respond to urgency and perform best under pressure, when the price of failure would be high. It is human nature to defer action until the need for it is clear and immediate. Generations of students have written their papers the night before they are due and many people file their income taxes just before midnight on April 15. Goals and deadlines motivate intensive and exceptional effort. Although it is not unusual for campaigns to be extended beyond their original deadline, sometimes with an increase in the goal, there is usually an end date in sight.

The financial needs of higher education institutions, while important, are usually related to long-term goals and are justified intellectually. While many people hold deep feelings for colleges and universities, their financial needs do not necessarily inspire the same emotion as true emergencies. For example, providing scholarships so that young people have educational opportunities and can become leaders in society is a goal of critical importance to the future. But it is generally not as urgently compelling as the scenes of homeless storm victims shown in the news during a disaster.

It is interesting to reflect on the fact that during the Covid-19 pandemic in 2020 and 2021, many donors responded to emergency appeals for funds to assist students facing hardships. That suggests that the immediacy of a need is an incentive to respond. Absent such a bona fide emergency, campaigns are designed to create urgency by establishing specific goals and deadlines for their achievement.

For a college or university, announcing a campaign goal and a deadline for its achievement raises the stakes. The reputation of the institution and its leaders is on the line. The risk of failure helps to motivate action, create excitement, and gain visibility—both for the campaign itself and for the substantive academic vision that it is intended to advance. Placing the institution's academic goals and related financial needs in the spotlight also reveals the magnitude of the overall effort and puts it in context, providing potential donors with a standard of appropriate response.

A fundraising effort that has no goal—for example, that is intended to "raise as much as we can" or that continues until a certain total has been achieved—is not really a campaign. It is perhaps a program or an initiative, but it does not meet the strict definition of a campaign. A goal and deadline that are known only to those within the institution may be motivating to them, but they do not necessarily influence the thinking of those from whom support is sought. That is perhaps more like a sales initiative than a campaign.

A campaign generally has a specific dollar goal and a deadline for achieving it that are announced to the public, in order to capture attention and motivate timely action by all whose participation is essential to its success.

Focus on Specific Purposes

While most comprehensive campaigns count all gifts and commitments during the campaign period toward the goal, they emphasize specific priorities. People give money to meet important needs or pursue exciting opportunities, not merely because they are asked to do so. Just "give"—or even "please give"—is not a very compelling request absent substantive reasons to do so. People respond to objectives that are concrete and not so much to generalities. They respond to lofty ideals, but also need to see the connection between the specific actions they are asked to take and how those ideals will be advanced. This is increasingly true, as many donors focus on the impact of their giving, a point that is discussed further later in this book.

Campaign priorities may be broadly defined, but they are determined up front as a part of campaign planning. Institutional strategic planning is usually undertaken in advance of a campaign in order to identify the institutional directions on which campaign priorities will be based. Indeed, as Zeidenstein (2019, p. 25) acknowledges, "[the] pattern of *strategic plan* → *institutional goals* → *campaign priorities* is now established orthodoxy. . . ."

But it is important to recognize that the path from strategic plan to campaign plan is interactive and iterative, not linear. The strategic plan may dictate the priorities that will be discussed with donors in the campaign, but in many cases knowledge about what donors value, and may support, also feeds back into the institutional planning process and influences the plan itself.

Campaign planning usually involves collecting information from and about prospective donors, in essence, market research. This may involve interviews, focus groups, surveys, and/or analysis of data on existing and prospective donors. Indeed, the use of sophisticated data analytics has become a hallmark of campaign planning. This information is also helpful in strategic planning.

If it is clear that some institutional priority is not attractive to donors—or that the institution's donor base does not have the capacity to fully support it—then another way of funding it may need to be considered. On the other hand, if there is strong donor interest in a particular project, and if the project is also consistent with the university's goals, then it may make sense to give it a higher priority in the plan. In some instances, the chief advancement officer participates in the strategic planning and is able to facilitate the iterative process of institutional and campaign planning (Webster, Jakeman, and Swayze, 2020). There are justifiable concerns about donor influence on institutional priorities, a point that is discussed further in the concluding chapter of this book.

Universities express their campaign priorities in a variety of ways. Some identify campaign priorities in terms of the *use of funds*: current support (annual fund); endowment (often specifying scholarships, professorships, and other purposes); and facilities projects. For example, Manhattan College announced a campaign in 2019 with priorities that included enhancing facilities, growing endowment for scholarships and faculty development, and securing unrestricted support for academic programming and student support services (McHugh, 2019).

Joslyn (2019b) observes that donors are increasingly demanding detailed information on the impact of their gifts, whether on the institution and its constituencies or on broader social purposes. For this reason, many campaigns define their priorities in terms of the impact that gifts can have rather than simply how the funds will be used.

Some campaigns emphasize the impact of the campaign *on the institution* itself. That may be defined in terms of its various constituencies, for example students and faculty, or certain activities, such as teaching and research. For example, Purdue University's campaign ("Ever True"), completed in 2019, included priorities in three categories: placing students first, building on our (institutional) strengths, and research and innovation. Specific objectives under these priorities included scholarship support, new professorships, support for research, facilities projects, and unrestricted support (annual giving) (Purdue University, n.d.). The University of California Berkeley's $6 billion campaign, launched in 2020, identified its priorities in terms of students and faculty, undergraduate opportunity and experience, research for the public good, and places of possibility (facilities) (University of California Berkeley, 2021).

In other instances, campaign goals are justified on the basis of how their achievement will enable the institution to increase its impact on society, for example by improving the environment or expanding medical knowledge. And some campaigns reflect a blend of these approaches, combining institutional purposes and social causes. For example, Ohio State's campaign underway in 2021 ("Time and Change") offered donors opportunities to support institutional priorities, including students and facilities, or "causes and interests." The latter included among others, animals, community, the environment, and global initiatives (Ohio State University, 2021). The University of Pennsylvania ("The Power of Penn") also identified campaign priorities including both institutional and social impact: expand student opportunities; advance knowledge across disciplines; revolutionize health; incubate innovation and entrepreneurship; drive energy solutions; engage Penn alumni; and create spaces that drive solutions (University of Pennsylvania, n.d.).

It has become common practice for campaign priorities to be based on broad themes, which are sometimes called "pillars." In some cases, campaign commitments are credited under one of these pillars, commonly also referred to as "buckets" (Gonzalez, 2021). More specific objectives, such as endowment or facilities projects, are often articulated under the over-arching themes or pillars, as are objectives related to specific schools and units. In some cases, the pillars are just marketing themes and gifts are credited under traditional categories, for example, annual giving or endowment. In other cases, gift commitments are recorded under one of the pillars, that is, added to one of the buckets. The latter can be complicated operationally, since it may not always be obvious into which bucket a particular gift should be added.

Emphasis on Principal and Major Gifts

Although comprehensive campaigns include annual giving, which produces many smaller gifts, they emphasize the principal and major gifts that will comprise the largest portion of funds raised toward the campaign's objectives. The definition of those terms is based on the dollar amount and may differ from one institution to another. It is common to define a major gift as $100,000 or more and a principal gift as a commitment of $1 million or more.

In past decades it was common to speak of the 80/20 rule, that is, the fact that about 80 percent of the campaign's total would result from about 20 percent of gifts. In the 1990s and 2000s, the results of many campaigns suggested that the rule had moved to something more like 90/10, with almost 90 percent of the total resulting from just 10 percent of gifts to the campaign. The trend appears to have continued; in one recent campaign at the University of Washington, 1 percent of the donors provided 92 percent of the funds raised (Thomas, 2021).

Campaigns are undertaken to raise the sights of donors across the board, but especially to secure the principal and major gifts that can have a significant, even transformational, impact on the institution and its programs.

Rated Prospect Lists and Specific Asks

Wealth and income are unevenly distributed. That has been true in every society has ever existed, but it is markedly true in the United States in the twenty-first century. That affects the ability of individuals to make philanthropic gifts.

Most people know where they stand in the economic hierarchy and also have an innate sense of fairness—a desire to do their fair share but also the expectation that others will do theirs as well. Despite its Marxist overtones, the idea of "from each according to their ability" is one with which most people agree with regard to giving.

Recognizing this social reality, campaign fundraising reflects the principle of proportionate giving, a term introduced by fundraising consultant Harold "Si" Seymour in the 1960s (Seymour, 1966). In other words, individuals are asked to give in proportion to their capacity to do so. But they are not asked simply to give what they can. That would not be a campaign, but rather a collection. In a campaign, the top prospects are asked for specific amounts for specific purposes, based on an assessment of their financial capabilities and interests.

A common misunderstanding is to think that fundraising can be undertaken according to the multiplication table, for example, that $1 million can be raised by soliciting $1,000 each from one thousand people. That always fails because it does not reflect the reality of disproportionate financial ability and the natural tendency of human beings—even if equally committed to the cause—to determine their fair share according to their perceptions of their relative economic standing in whatever community may be relevant. In a comprehensive campaign that includes annual giving, many small gifts will comprise some portion of the overall total that is attained. But significant goals require substantial principal and major gifts, and preparing for a campaign includes identifying prospects financially capable of such gifts.

The gift table, sometimes called the "gift chart" or "gift-range chart," illustrates the number and level of gifts that a certain dollar goal will require. Based on typical patterns achieved in many completed campaigns, it can be used as a tool for planning a campaign and for tracking its progress along the way.

Table 1.1 provides an example of a gift table based on a hypothetical goal of $250 million. It must be emphasized that this table reflects *traditional assumptions*, including: a lead gift equivalent to 10 percent of the goal; the ten largest gifts producing one-third of the goal; 100 gifts producing the next one-third of the goal; and gifts at lower levels producing the final one-third of the goal. It may offer a *starting point* for planning, but a table constructed according to these traditional assumptions is almost certainly not realistic for most campaigns today.

For one thing, as mentioned previously, the trend is toward a smaller number of gifts accounting for a larger percentage of the total raised. Moreover, any table developed using some type of formula is unlikely to be relevant to

Table 1.1. Traditional Gift Table for $250 Million Goal

Gift Range	No. of Gifts Required	Total at This Level	Cumulative Total	Cumulative Percentage of Goal
$25,000,000	1	$25,000,000	$25,000,000	10%
10,000,000	3	30,000,000	55,000,000	22%
5,000,000	6	30,000,000	85,000,000	34%
2,500,000	12	30,000,000	115,000,000	46%
1,000,000	27	27,000,000	142,000,000	57%
500,000	52	26,000,000	168,000,000	67%
250,000	100	25,000,000	193,000,000	77%
100,000	180	18,000,000	211,000,000	84%
50,000	300	15,000,000	226,000,000	90%
25,000	560	14,000,000	240,000,000	96%
<25,000	Many	10,000,000	$250,000,000	100%

Note: This table reflects traditional assumptions. It may serve as a starting point for developing a gift table for a specific campaign, but would need to be altered to reflect today's trends and the realities of a particular institution.

a particular institution; the table needs to be based on a realistic assessment of the university's donor prospects and the likelihood that donors will respond at the levels they are believed to be capable of giving. For example, if the institution has identified a potential gift of $50 million in its $250 million campaign, it would make no sense to develop a gift table that starts at half that amount. The traditional table depicted in Table 1.1 needs to be adjusted in light of the realities of the institution's constituency, fundraising history, and other information developed through analysis.

Developing a gift table is an essential step in planning a campaign and it helps to bring a sense of reality to setting a preliminary campaign goal. Some may be tempted to set a goal that is simply higher than the university's previous campaign or higher than the campaign goal of some peer or rival institution. But when the proposed goal is analyzed in terms of the number and level of gifts that would be required to achieve it, and compared to what is known about the institution's existing donor constituency, the result may reframe the discussion along more realistic lines. It is fine for a university to stretch in setting a goal, but it is obviously risky to do so based on hope. As Charles Phlegar (2021, p. 27), vice president at Virginia Tech, states it, "The institution's goals . . . must be on the edge of feasibility without losing credibility."

Sequential Fundraising

Again, most people want to do what is fair and what is expected of them. And they tend to look to the behavior of others to determine what that means. Accordingly, a traditional campaign follows a process that starts with the solicitation of those deemed capable of the largest commitments and those who are closest to the institution—those who are seen as having the greatest stake in the campaign's success. This approach is sometimes described as solicitation "from top down and the inside out" and is known as "sequential fundraising," a term commonly attributed to the legendary campaign consultant George Brakeley Jr. (McGoldrick and Robell, 2002, p. 141).

Following this principle, among the first people solicited usually are members of the institution's governing board (and/or the board of its affiliated foundation) and the most highly capable and committed gift prospects. Established regular donors and prospective donors who are deemed to have significant capacity and interest also are solicited early in the process. Following the inside-out principle, the faculty and staff are often solicited early in the campaign. They may not be top prospects in terms of their financial capacity, but they are clearly among the closest members of the campus family. The top-down/inside-out process unfolds over the course of the campaign, and discipline in following it is important to maximize support.

Except for the annual giving program, which continues throughout a comprehensive campaign, a fundraising effort that begins with a broad solicitation of the institution's entire constituency is not a campaign. It is an appeal. It is unlikely to maximize giving because it does not provide those who are asked with any standards to judge what their own response should be. The top prospects and campaign insiders have the opportunity to leverage the impact of their gifts through their influence on the giving of others within the constituency, or to jeopardize the entire effort with a disappointing response.

While sequential fundraising remains a useful principle, for the reasons discussed, it must be acknowledged that it may be less relevant in many contemporary campaigns that extend over a long period of years, as many do. There may be prospective donors who are capable of principal and major gifts who have not been identified at the outset of the campaign. Or it may require a long period of time to develop relationships with them and their gifts may not mature until a later phase of the campaign. In addition, donors who are motivated by the impact of their gifts on the institution or a social cause may not be influenced so much by what others have given as by the depth of their own commitment.

The relevance of the sequential approach also may vary among institutions and constituencies. For example, it may be highly relevant within the governing board or foundation board. People know each other and have a sense of their relative economic standing. A disappointing gift from a member known to be wealthy may have a negative impact on the decisions of other board members. Or a particularly generous commitment from one board member may inspire others to consider larger gifts. On the other hand, for a large institution with a national donor base and a case for support built around social impact, donors may be less influenced by what others have given.

But many people still do look to the example of what others have done in determining their own gift. It is for that reason that principal and major gifts are revealed and publicized, often at the time a campaign is publicly announced. The continuing success of challenge gifts as a fundraising strategy also suggests that many donors still respond to the examples and standards established by others. And, it is interesting to observe, that many crowdfunding campaigns on social media show the amounts given by specific donors and some who respond may determine the amount of their gifts by comparison with others. So new methods of fundraising may still tap into some traditional aspects of human nature.

Proceeding in Phases

Campaigns proceed in definable phases, most commonly as depicted in Figure 1.1. It is important to note that some authors have proposed new

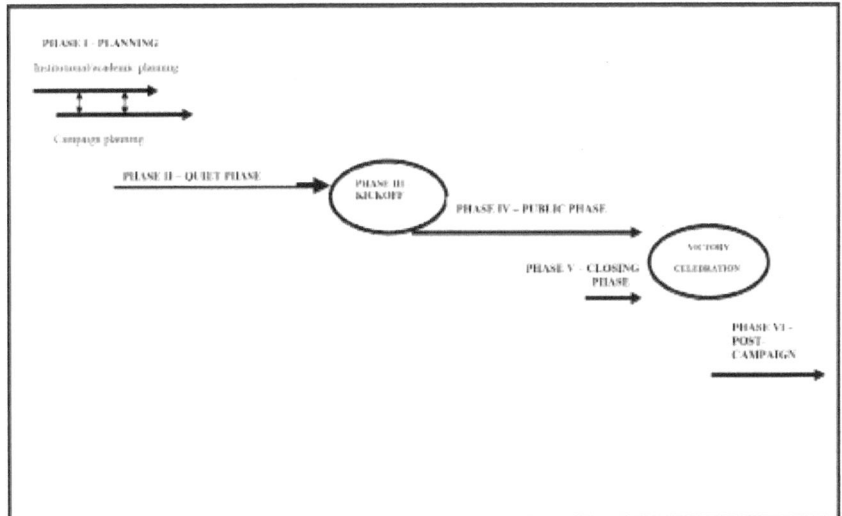

Figure 1.1. Phases of the Campaign. *Worth, Michael J. 2017.* Leading the Campaign: The President and Fundraising in Higher Education *(2nd edition). Lanham, MD: Rowman & Littlefield, p. 24.*

models for the phases of a campaign (e.g., Langley, 2016), but most represent variations on the traditional phases as shown in Figure 1.1.

Preparation for a campaign begins with planning at two levels. The institution needs to engage in strategic planning to establish its academic directions, priorities, and substantive goals for the future and identify the financial resources necessary to achieving them. At the same time, the development office or the foundation will be planning with a more specific focus on the steps necessary to attain campaign readiness.

As mentioned previously, and as Figure 1.1 suggests, academic goals identified through institutional planning shape the campaign priorities and objectives, while realistic assessments of the potential for fundraising need to be reflected in the institutional plan. As stated previously, the processes are interactive and iterative. Chief advancement officers are often involved in the university's strategic planning, bringing insights on the philanthropic market to the consideration of institutional strategies (Hinton, 2012).

Some institutions undertake a participative strategic planning process, including various constituencies and including surveys, focus groups, and other practices. However, it is also possible to identify strategic plans that appear to be based largely on the vision of a president. The advantage of a participative process is that it may help to build consensus and support for the directions that are identified, but of course, it also can consume time and resources that some may consider excessive.

Campaign planning may include retaining a consultant to conduct a campaign planning study, historically known as a "feasibility study." The latter term is somewhat out of date now and the term "campaign planning study" is more commonly used. The idea of feasibility was highly relevant when universities were conducting campaigns to fund specific capital projects; if the campaign was not feasible, neither was the project. But in a comprehensive campaign, the question is not really whether the institution can have a campaign, but rather what goal and timetable may be most realistic and which priorities may be more or less attractive to donors.

Campaign planning studies may involve engaging a consultant to conduct meetings with prospective donors, individually or in focus groups, in which preliminary campaign priorities are discussed. These interviews are confidential and the candid reactions of interview participants may provide the campaign planners with important insights. This is still a common practice, but larger institutions with well-developed programs and strong relationships with donors may undertake their own planning study and some employ a hybrid approach that includes staff meetings with prospective donors as well as some interviews done by consultants (Sowell and Schroeder, 2021).

Most campaign planning studies also make important use of data analytics, in which the university's fundraising history and donor characteristics provide guidance on what may be realistic and also suggest strategies for structuring the campaign. Indeed, the growing sophistication of data analytics is a hallmark of principal and major gifts fundraising today.

Once campaign priorities have been identified, the campaign enters a "quiet phase," which is sometimes called the "silent phase." The former term is more accurate. While the campaign has not yet been publicly announced during this phase, there are a number of people who are aware that it is underway, so it really is more quiet than silent. This book uses "quiet phase" except in quoting a source that uses the alternative.

The quiet phase may continue for a period of years, in order to assure appropriate attention to top prospects and insiders before the campaign is announced to the broader constituency. Solicitations undertaken during the quiet phase also provide a test of the priorities and themes, allowing for possible adjustments before the campaign and its goal are announced. Langley (2016) uses the term "pilot phase," which may indeed be more descriptive of what occurs during this period than the traditional label quiet phase.

Once the quiet phase has produced commitments totaling a substantial portion of the ultimate campaign goal—commonly between 30 and 50 percent—the campaign is announced and enters its public phase (Schroeder, 2019, p. 17). However, some campaigns are announced with much less in commitments and others wait to attain a larger total before formally entering the public phase. Case studies included in this book provide examples of both approaches.

Gift commitments secured during the quiet phase comprise the "nucleus fund" for the campaign. The public announcement of the campaign is almost always a highly publicized event, called the "kickoff," at which the campaign's goal is revealed, its priorities and themes are highlighted, and the top donors during the quiet phase are recognized.

The public phase continues until the campaign is concluded. Some identify the campaign's final year or so as a distinctive phase, called a "closing" or "wrap-up" phase. This may include efforts to broaden the base of support and/or may include some refocusing on campaign objectives that have not yet been achieved. Some authors also include a post-campaign phase as an important part of the process. A careful analysis of the campaign, sometimes undertaken by a consultant, provides important lessons and may be the first step in preparing for the next campaign.

The process is important. The quiet phase provides incentives to top donors to stretch their gifts, recognizing that—according to the principle of proportionate giving—they will establish an example for others to follow. Rolling out the campaign prematurely runs the risk of preemptive gifts that lower the standards for the duration. Announcing a goal too soon also runs the risk that the institution has over-estimated potential support and set its sights too high;

that risk is greatly reduced if a substantial portion of the goal has been committed before the public announcement of the goal and deadline takes place.

Having a substantial nucleus fund also may offer assurance to donors who will be approached during the public phase of the campaign. Few donors would be willing to commit to achieving a vision that may seem ambitious unless they believe that it can indeed be accomplished. Announcement of a campaign with a substantial nucleus fund thus makes the goals and priorities seem doable; that assures that donors will be joining a winning effort. Charles Phlegar's (2021, p. 27) point, mentioned earlier, bears repeating: "The institution's goals . . . must be on the edge of feasibility without losing credibility."

Use of Organized Volunteer Leadership

People support institutions and causes with which they are involved. And people follow the example of others whom they admire and respect. They wish to be associated with others who are viewed as successful and worthy individuals and not with those whose reputations do not impress them. They tend to discount assertions by those with obvious self-interest and to seek reassurance in the endorsement of others who have no personal stake in the matter.

That is why people are selective about who they accept as a friend or contact on social networking sites and why political candidates seek the endorsements of others who are well regarded within their communities or parties. That is why consumers give greater credibility to the reviews of fellow consumers than to the representations of advertising or salespersons. These tendencies of human nature with regard to fundraising and giving are supported by academic research as well as practitioner experience (Lindahl, 2010, pp. 85–105).

A campaign is led by prominent volunteers, whose own prestige and credibility authenticate the institution and its goals. Their visible involvement makes a statement about the importance of the college or university and the worthiness of its campaign. They make it attractive for others who are like them, or who aspire to be, to participate with them in the campaign, through giving and in other ways.

In some cases, volunteer leaders may be involved in planning and execution of the campaign. Indeed, in research for his 2015 doctoral dissertation, Robert Rhodes Logan studied two campaigns and concluded that volunteer leaders actually had been more influential in setting the campaign goals than were the consultants hired to assess feasibility (Logan, 2015). The cases in this book reveal instances in which volunteers are actively involved in identifying and soliciting donors; however, in other cases, the role of volunteer leaders is largely honorary. Their role may be to provide a public face of the campaign, but not to be deeply involved in planning or execution.

In reality, many campaign gifts are solicited by the president, other academic officers, and development or advancement staff members. Indeed, many campaigns today are primarily staff-driven, especially at research universities with large development offices. The number of solicitations required to achieve a big campaign goal and the complexity of some gift arrangements often dictate that professional gift officers play the central role. In those circumstances, volunteers may not go much beyond providing symbolic leadership and perhaps opening doors to new donors.

Most presidents are actively engaged in cultivating donors and soliciting gifts, often accompanied by their chief development officers. Some authors point to the paramount importance of the president's leadership (Worth, 2017). One academic study highlights how turnover in that office can present challenges for an ongoing campaign (Nehls, 2008). And, as mentioned previously, some speculate that shorter presidential terms may eventually lead to shorter campaigns (Schroeder, 2019).

Campaign volunteer leadership often is organized in a structure, usually including a chair or co-chairs, a campaign executive committee (which may be identified by various other terms), and perhaps committees focused on various academic units, donor constituencies, geographic regions, or particular campaign priorities. In other cases, the volunteer structure is kept lean, with overall monitoring of the campaign provided by the governing board's standing committee on advancement or development.

Integrated with the Institution's Marketing, Branding, and Engagement Strategies

As mentioned previously, comprehensive campaigns today are about more than raising money. They are usually integrated with broader marketing and communication themes designed to increase the visibility of the college or university and enhance its brand. These themes often establish the pillars under which campaign priorities are described.

As Schroeder (2019, p. 121) explains, "Campaigns provide institutions with wonderful opportunities for storytelling and moments to amplify the aspirations of an institutions particular direction and trajectory, as well as the role of philanthropic and volunteer partners." Indeed, some institutions have successfully used campaigns to align their brands across the critical constituencies of students, alumni, and donors (Sevilla, 2018).

Alumni participation in giving has declined in recent decades across higher education. The engagement of new donors, that is, building the pipeline for the future, is a high priority for many universities. The visibility and excitement of a campaign may provide the environment for increasing alumni engagement and participation and such non-monetary goals are explicit in some campaigns. For examples, William & Mary's campaign, "For the Bold," included the goal of increasing alumni participation to 40 percent by 2020 ("For the Bold," 2021).

CAMPAIGNS TODAY

As discussed earlier in this chapter, college and university campaigns have evolved over the many decades since they were first introduced. The final chapter of this book includes some speculation about the future. But where are we today—or at least, where were we before the onset of the Covid-19 pandemic in 2020?

In 2017—following the nation's recovery from the Great Recession but before the onset of the pandemic—the fundraising consulting firm BWF noted some prominent campaign trends, including the continuing importance of the top 1 percent of gifts; the continuing rise in campaign goals; and lengthening campaigns. Although the number of alumni donors has declined overall, principal and major gifts from alumni were accounting for an increasing percentage of campaign totals. And advancement staffs were growing, reflecting the critical importance of campaigns as part of institutional strategies (BWF, 2017).

The following year, the marketing consulting firm Ruffalo Noel Levitz (2018) conducted a survey of 598 chief advancement officers and reported five key findings. By this report, perpetual campaigns—meaning that counting toward the new campaign continues uninterrupted from conclusion of the previous one—had become the norm. Campaigns were encompassing an even wider range of priorities, including permanent and current support. Gearing up for a campaign required more resources, with advancement budgets increasing by 65 percent on average. New channels, new donors, and productivity had become top areas of focus. And, unsurprisingly, advancement officers reported that meeting campaign goals and providing a positive donor experience were their top priorities.

Significantly, while gift officer contact remained the most important method of soliciting in 2018, new channels of communication, including digital outreach, were becoming more important, and emerging technology, including productivity tools, were changing the nature of campaign management (Ruffalo Noel Levitz, 2018). Then Covid-19 hit the nation and the world. Campuses closed down, instruction became remote, travel for in-person meetings became unsafe and, for most donors, unwelcome. Universities and their campaigns needed to adapt.

As described in the case studies in following chapters of this book, universities greatly increased the use of videoconferencing, virtual events, and creative applications of email, phone, and other communication channels, as well as new systems for identifying prospects and managing donor interactions (Jackson, 2020). Both gift officers and donors learned how to use new technologies to communicate and maintain relationships, developing skills and habits that may represent permanent changes in how fundraising is conducted.

The campaigns discussed in the following chapters of this book were all underway during the pandemic and each case includes references to how the institution adapted to that reality. But the impact of Covid-19 is not a major focus of this book. Some of the new methods developed during the pandemic may represent permanent changes, while perhaps more traditional practices will regain ground.

The concluding chapter of this book highlights some notable features of the campaigns discussed in the intervening chapters and summarizes some predictions about the future of campaigns. There are pros and cons to the campaign model as we have known it and some argue that campaigns are not always, or perhaps ever, the best fundraising approach for a college or university. Others see a continuing role for campaigns, but suggest new models and definitions.

This book is based on two basic assumptions: Comprehensive campaigns will continue to be a critical strategy for advancing colleges and universities. And they will continue to evolve, employing new strategies and methods, some of which are illustrated in the case studies that follow.

NOTE: Some sections of this chapter are adapted from Worth, Michael J. 2017. *Leading the Campaign: The President and Fundraising in Higher Education.* Lanham, MD: Rowman & Littlefield.

REFERENCES

BWF. 2017. *Fundraising Campaign Trends.* https://www.bwf.com/alumni-relations/fundraising-campaign-trends/ (accessed April 6, 2021).

Council for Advancement and Support of Education (CASE). 2013. *CASE Campaign Report.* Washington, DC: Author.

Council for Advancement and Support of Education (CASE). 2021. *CASE Global Reporting Standards.* Washington, DC: Author.

Cutlip, Scott M. 1965. *Fund Raising in the United States: Its Role in American Philanthropy.* New Brunswick, NJ: Rutgers University Press.

Dove, Kent E. 2000. *Conducting a Successful Capital Campaign* (2nd edition). San Francisco: Jossey-Bass.

Eynon, Matthew and Brian Hastings. 2021. "Reporting Campaign Gifts: Transparency Counts" (Chapter 5). In *Fundraising Campaigns in Higher Education: A Practical Guide for Governing and Foundation Boards*, edited by John Lippincott and Tom Mitchell, 103–115. Washington, DC: Association of Governing Boards of Universities and Colleges.

For the Bold. 2021. Website. https://forthebold.wm.edu/about/ (accessed February 4, 2021).

Gonzalez, Sergio. 2021. "Framing the Campaign: Strategy, Structure, and Discipline" (Chapter 3). In *Fundraising Campaigns in Higher Education: A Practical Guide for Governing and Foundation Boards*, edited by John Lippincott and Tom Mitchell, 70–86. Washington, DC: Association of Governing Boards of Universities and Colleges.

Guillaume, Kristine E. and Jamie D. Halper. 2018. "Harvard Raises $9.6 Billion in Final Capital Campaign Tally, Smashing Its Own Fundraising Record." *Harvard Crimson*, September 20. https://www.thecrimson.com/article/2018/9/20/capital-campaign-final-figure/ (accessed November 18, 2020).

Hinton, Karen E. 2012. *A Practical Guide to Strategic Planning in Higher Education*. Ann Arbor, MI: Society for College and University Planning. http://blogs.nwic.edu/strategicplan/files/2016/04/Guide_Strategic-Planning_Higher-Ed_Hinton.pdf

Jackson, Nancy. 2020. "3 New Higher-Ed Fundraising Trends That Should Last." *Chronicle of Philanthropy*, June 18. www.philanthropy.com (accessed November 18, 2020).

Joslyn, Heather. 2019a. "The Benefits of a 'Blended' Campaign." *Chronicle of Philanthropy*, April 2. www.philanthropy.com. (accessed December 23, 2020).

Joslyn, Heather. 2019b. "It's Almost a Requirement Now to Tell Donors the Impact of Their Gifts." *Chronicle of Philanthropy*, April 2. (accessed December 23, 2020).

Kell, Gretchen. 2020. "UC Berkeley Launches Landmark $6 Billion Fundraising Campaign." *Berkeley News*, February 29. https://news.berkeley.edu/2020/02/29/berkeley-launches-6-billion-light-the-way-fundraiser/#:~:text=The%20University%20of%20California%2C%20Berkeley,by%20the%20end%20of%202023 (accessed November 18, 2020).

Langley, James M. 2016. *Comprehensive Fundraising Campaigns: A Guide for Presidents and Boards*. Denver, CO: Academic Impressions.

Lindahl, Wesley E. 2010. *Principles of Fundraising: Theory and Practice*. Sudbury, MA: Jones and Bartlett Publishers.

Logan, William Rhodes. 2015. *The Factors That Influenced the Decision to Enter Into a $1 billion Fundraising Campaign by Two Public Higher Education Institutions*. Dissertation, University of Tennessee-Knoxville. https://trace.tennessee.edu/utk_graddiss/3347/ (accessed March 8, 2021).

McGoldrick, William P., and Paul A. Robell. 2002. "Campaigning in the New Century." In *New Strategies for Educational Fund Raising*, edited by Michael J. Worth, 135–152. Westport, CT: American Council on Education and Praeger.

McHugh, Pete. 2019. "Manhattan College Celebrates Public Launch of Capital Campaign." Press release, September 19. https://manhattan.edu/news/archive/2019/09/invest-in-the-vision-capital-campaign-launch.php (accessed April 6, 2021).

Nehls, Kimberly. 2008. "Raising the Cash: A Study of the Role of Leadership in a Capital Campaign." *Higher Education,* 37 (2), 89–103.

The Ohio State University. 2021. Time and Change: The Ohio State Campaign (Website). https://campaign.osu.edu/giving-opportunities/support-your-passion/ (accessed April 6, 2021).

Phlegar, Charles D. 2021. "First Things First: Institutional Mission, Values, and Strategic Plan" (Chapter 1). In *Fundraising Campaigns in Higher Education: A Practical Guide for Governing and Foundation Boards*, edited by John Lippincott and Tom Mitchell, 19–40. Washington, DC: Association of Governing Boards of Universities and Colleges.

Purdue University. n.d. Ever True. (Website) https://www.purdue.edu/evertrue/faqs.html (accessed April 6, 2021).

Ruffalo Noel Levitz. 2018. *Advancement Leaders Speak: The Future of Higher Education Fundraising Campaigns*. Cedar Rapids, Iowa: author.

Schroeder, Fritz W. 2019. "The Art and Science of Comprehensive Campaigns." In *Advancing Higher Education: New Strategies for Fundraising, Philanthropy, and Engagement*, edited by Michael J. Worth and Matthew T. Lambert, 113–128. Lanham, MD: Rowman & Littlefield.

Sevilla, Ed. 2018. "Best practices for aligning university brands with fundraising campaigns." *Journal of Brand Strategy*, 7 (1), Summer, 69–83.

Seymour, Harold J. 1966. *Designs for Fund-raising*. New York: McGraw-Hill.

Sowell, Ashlyn W. and Fritz W. Schroeder. 2021. "Preparing for the Campaign: Setting Priorities and Assessing Readiness" (Chapter 2). In *Fundraising Campaigns in Higher Education: A Practical Guide for Governing and Foundation Boards*, edited by John Lippincott and Tom Mitchell, 41–69. Washington, DC: Association of Governing Boards of Universities and Colleges.

Thomas, Lisa. 2021. "Campaign Stakeholders: Profound Engagement" (Chapter 9). In *Fundraising Campaigns in Higher Education: A Practical Guide for Governing and Foundation Boards*, edited by John Lippincott and Tom Mitchell, 180–200. Washington, DC: Association of Governing Boards of Universities and Colleges.

University of California Berkeley. 2021. Light the Way. (Website) https://light.berkeley.edu/ (accessed April 6, 2021).

University of Pennsylvania. n.d. The Power of Penn. (Website) https://powerofpenn.upenn.edu/ (accessed April 6, 2021).

Webster, Wayne P., Rick C. Jakeman, and Susan Swayze. 2020. "The Role of Philanthropy on the Strategic Planning Process of a Selective Liberal Arts and Science College." In *Start-Ups and SMEs: Concepts, Methodologies, Tools, and Applications*, edited by Information Resources Management Association, 1364–1384. Hershey, PA: IGI Global. http://doi:10.4018/978-1-7998-1760-4.ch070

Worth, Michael J. 2017. *Leading the Campaign: The President and Fundraising in Higher Education*. Lanham, MD: Rowman & Littlefield.

Xia, Karen. 2018. "Bollinger's fundraising for Columbia has set records. What do his methods mean for the University's future?" *Columbia Spectator*, October 25. https://www.columbiaspectator.com/news/2018/10/25/bollingers-fundraising-for-columbia-has-set-records-what-do-his-methods-mean-for-the-universitys-future/ (accessed November 16, 2020).

Zeidenstein, Darrow. 2019. "Strategy as the Foundation for Advancement." In *Advancing Higher Education: New Strategies for Fundraising, Philanthropy, and Engagement*, edited by Michael J. Worth and Matthew T. Lambert, 25–34. Lanham, MD: Rowman & Littlefield.

PART I

Doctoral Universities

In the Carnegie Classification of Institutions of Higher Education, Doctoral Universities are identified in three categories, based on the number of research-oriented degrees awarded and total research expenditures. Those with the very highest research activity are classified as Research-1 (R1) and those with high research activity are classified as Research-2 (R2). Beginning in 2019, a new category of Doctoral/Professional (D/PU) was created to include universities that offer professional practice doctoral degrees, for example, the M.D., J.D. or D. Div., but that are not significantly focused on research.

Particularly with regard to doctoral universities, some express a concern that the Carnegie classifications are sometimes interpreted as "rankings," rather than simply groupings of institutions by the nature of their activities (Toppo, 2018). Indeed, some states use the term "Tier 1" instead of "Research-1," implying a ranking that the Carnegie classifications do not intend (Borden, 2021).

Doctoral universities include many of the best known institutions in the country. These institutions have significant advantages in fundraising. Many have large enrollments, especially flagship state university campuses, which may increase the odds that their alumni bodies will include individuals who are wealthy and philanthropic. Their wide range of programs offers multiple giving opportunities that may coincide with donor interests and priorities. And their research is often related to broader social goals, such as medical advances or new technology, which may attract the support of donors committed to those purposes. On the other hand, large campuses may not inspire the same loyalty as smaller colleges; alumni participation rates are generally lower at large research universities than at more intimate, especially private, institutions.

The following three chapters include case studies of comprehensive campaigns at three doctoral universities: the Rochester Institute of Technology (R2), Tulane University (R1), and the University of Virginia (R1).

ROCHESTER INSTITUTE OF TECHNOLOGY (RIT)

The Rochester Institute of Technology (RIT) was classified as a master's degree institution in the Carnegie Classification of Institutions of Higher Education until 2016, when it became classified as Research-2, indicating high research activity. That change meant it would compete in a new league, driving an emphasis on obtaining support for research. Consistent with that priority, in 2018 it announced "The Campaign for Greatness," with a $1 billion goal. It was identified as a "blended campaign," meaning that funds counted toward the goal would include not only traditional philanthropic commitments but also support from government, corporate partners, and research foundations and agencies. This strategy was intended to encourage private donors to make gifts for research, which might be leveraged by combining them with funds from other sources.

TULANE UNIVERSITY

In 2005, Tulane University was devastated by Hurricane Katrina, the worst natural disaster in the nation's history to that time. For nearly the next decade, the university was focused on survival, recovery, and renewal. With the arrival of a new president in 2014, Tulane was ready to pivot to a new era, focused on expanded ambitions for research and impact. In 2017, it launched "Only the Audacious," a $1.3 billion campaign integrated with an overall marketing strategy intended to move the university and the city past the residual trauma of Katrina. The goal was to move past the mindset of "doing more with less," which the Katrina experience had fostered, into a new attitude of boldness and ambition for "doing more with more" (Wise, 2021).

UNIVERSITY OF VIRGINIA

The University of Virginia (UVA) is among the oldest and most highly regarded public universities in the nation, with a long record of successful campaigns. Having surpassed the $3 billion goal of its previous campaign in 2013 and with a presidential transition on the horizon, UVA desired to maintain its momentum and transparency. It just kept campaigning. All gifts made since the close of the previous campaign would be counted toward the new campaign, "Honor the Future," essentially placing UVA in a perpetual campaign mode. Departing from the traditional practice of not announcing a campaign until the quiet phase has been completed, in 2018 UVA made public the fact that it was planning a new campaign, that the goal would be $5 billion, and that it would be formally announced *a year later*, in connection with the university's bicentennial.

REFERENCES

Borden, Victor M.H. 2021. (Professor of Higher Education and Student Affairs, Project Director, Carnegie Classification of Institutions of Higher Education, Indiana University School of Education). Email to author, May 19, 2021.

Toppo, Greg 2018. "Universe of Doctoral Universities Expands." *Inside Higher Ed*, December 19. https://www.insidehighered.com/news/2018/12/19/professional-practice-doctoral-category-expands-carnegie-system (accessed May 18, 2021).

Wise, Ginny. 2021. Interview with author, May 11, 2021.

Chapter 2
Rochester Institute of Technology

TRANSFORMING RIT: THE CAMPAIGN FOR GREATNESS

The Rochester Institute of Technology (RIT) is a private university, located in Henrietta, New York, near the city of Rochester. RIT was originally located in downtown Rochester, the historic headquarters of Eastman Kodak (now called just "Kodak"), where one of its early benefactors was George Eastman, the founder of the company. In 1968, RIT moved to a newly constructed campus in Henrietta, sometimes referred to as "Brick City," a nickname related to the 15,710,693 bricks used in its construction ("Celebrating 50 Years at the Henrietta Campus," 2018). In addition to its main campus, RIT also maintains campuses in China, Croatia, and United Arab Emirates (Dubai).

RIT traces its founding to the establishment of the Rochester Athenaeum in 1829. The Athenaeum was a literary society created by local citizens, including Colonel Nathaniel Rochester, a revolutionary war soldier for whom the city is named. A separate technical training institution, the Mechanics Institute, was founded in 1885. The two institutions merged in 1891 and the combined entity was eventually renamed the Rochester Institute of Technology in 1944 (Rochester Institute of Technology, n.d.-a).

RIT enrolls 19,000 students in nine colleges, including liberal arts, art and design, and business, although it is especially known for science and engineering. It is also recognized for experiential learning, having been ranked eleventh for co-op and internship programs by U.S. News & World Report (Rochester Institute of Technology, n.d.-b). Distinctive among the colleges is The National Technical Institute for the Deaf, the first and largest technical college for deaf and hard-of-hearing students (Rochester Institute of Technology, n.d.-c).

Until 2016, RIT was classified as a Masters-Comprehensive institution in the Carnegie Classification of Institutions of Higher Education. It began to offer doctoral programs only in the 1980s, but by 2016, RIT had become re-designated as a doctoral university, with the Carnegie classification of

Research-2, indicating high research activity (Mozer, 2016). The change would begin a new era for RIT and significantly influence the strategy for a new campaign.

ADVANCEMENT AT RIT

Lisa Cauda joined RIT as associate vice president for development in 2000, after serving for nine years at the Stevens Institute of Technology. In 2005, she succeeded Laurel Price Jones as RIT's vice president for development and alumni relations when Price Jones moved to the vice presidency at the George Washington University (Finnerty, 2006a). After launching the public phase of a new campaign, Cauda transitioned to the role of vice president and secretary of the institute, working closely with the governing board. Phillip Castleberry was recruited from the vice presidency at St. John Fisher College to take over from Cauda as vice president for development and alumni relations (Finnerty, 2020a).

Arriving at RIT in 2020, Castleberry assumed responsibility for an ongoing campaign but also immediately began looking to the longer term. He changed the name of his division from development and alumni relations to University Advancement. As he explained, the change recognized the reality that "our focus extends far beyond fundraising and involves a constituency much larger than alumni" (Finnerty, 2020b).

While planning for completion of the comprehensive campaign that was underway, Castleberry also began to prepare for what would come next. He completed a staff reorganization, increasing the number of unit-based gift officers and creating a new central regional major gifts program, while maintaining direct oversight of principal gifts. He also established and launched a new leadership annual giving program, the Sentinel Society (Rochester Institute of Technology, 2021).

History of Campaigns

RIT has a history of comprehensive campaigns. "Access to the Future" was launched in 1985 and concluded in 1990, having raised $125 million against its $85 million goal (Rochester Institute of Technology 175th Anniversary, 2004). Albert Simone became president of RIT soon after completion of that campaign and initiated a process of institutional strategic planning.

The quiet phase of a new campaign based on Simone's plan began in 1998. Announced in 2002, "Powered by the Future: The Campaign for RIT" had a goal of $300 million, the largest in RIT's history to that time. The campaign was comprehensive, with priorities that emphasized endowment and facilities and included goals for each academic unit as well as university-wide purposes (Powered by the Future, 2002). The campaign was successfully concluded in 2006, with $309 million in gifts and commitments (Finnerty, 2006b).

GREATNESS THROUGH DIFFERENCE: THE RIT STRATEGIC PLAN 2018–2025

William W. Destler served as RIT's president from 2007 to 2017, having come from the position of provost and senior vice president at the University of Maryland. Research activity increased significantly under Destler's leadership, culminating in the designation as a research university in 2016. Destler also initiated a comprehensive strategic planning process, which led to a new plan, unveiled to the university community in 2014, and presided over the early phases of a new campaign (Dougherty, 2014).

Destler retired and was succeeded in 2017 by David C. Munson Jr. Former dean of the University of Michigan's engineering school, Munson was committed to continuing RIT's growth as a research institution, while maintaining its historic emphasis on students. His goal, he said, was "for RIT to be the most student-centered research university in the nation" (Goodman, 2017).

Munson quickly launched a collaborative 14-month strategic planning effort, building on the existing plan. The process culminated in "Greatness Through Difference: The RIT Strategic Plan 2018–2025," which was approved by the board of trustees in 2018.

The updated plan identified 25 specific goals to be achieved by 2025 on four dimensions:

- People (including support for students, faculty, staff, and alumni engagement)
- Programs (including an increase in doctoral programs, research, artistic activity, and experiential learning)
- Places (including several new or expanded facilities and achievement of carbon neutrality by 2030)
- Partnerships (including relationships focused on regional economic development, expanded health care programs, global partnerships, and expansion of Regional STEM Centers run by the National Technical Institute for the Deaf) (Rochester Institute of Technology, n.d.-d)

The plan developed under Destler and Munson called for an emphasis on expanding partnerships with the business community and government, and on regional economic growth. That would require resources going beyond those traditionally coming from philanthropy and set the stage for an unusual approach to RIT's comprehensive campaign.

TRANSFORMING RIT: THE CAMPAIGN FOR GREATNESS

In July 2018, President Munson announced to a crowd of nearly 2,000, supplemented by an equal number viewing online, that RIT was launching the largest campaign in its history, with a goal of $1 billion. The gala kickoff event featured international recording artist Nicole Henry, Broadway stars Beverly and Kirby Ward, and a humorous skit based on *The Wizard of Oz*, starring President Munson as the "Wizard of Bricks," a play on the campus nickname (Rosen, Moser, and McGrain, 2018).

The Campaign for Greatness would be a *blended campaign*—counting toward its goal not just traditional philanthropic commitments but also "support from a variety of investors, including alumni, government and corporate partners, and research foundations and agencies" (Rosen, Mozer, and McGrain, 2018).

Gifts totaling $530 million, made since 2013, would be counted toward the goal of the campaign, initially scheduled to conclude by 2022. The nucleus fund announced at the kickoff event included the largest gift RIT had ever received, $50 million from alumnus Austin McChord (Rosen, Mozer, and McGrain, 2018).

McChord, a member of the RIT board of trustees, had graduated from RIT in 2009 and founded Datto, a Connecticut-based data protection company with engineering and support offices in downtown Rochester. In the tradition of other technology entrepreneurs, he had started the company in his father's basement in 2007, based on an idea he developed while an RIT student. The company was later acquired and merged, with McChord remaining as CEO, and by 2015 was valued at more than $1 billion (Rosen, 2017).

McChord's gift supported a variety of purposes, including the Innovative Maker and Learning Complex, a new facility connecting RIT's Wallace Library and the Student Alumni Union, and housing programs in technology, art, and design. As discussed later in this study, his gift played a key role in some partnerships that defined the campaign's blended approach.

Campaign Priorities

Priorities of the campaign are summarized in Box 2.1 and are organized under four categories, identified as "pillars," including: attract exceptional talent (goal $200 million); enhance the student experience (goal $280 million);

BOX 2.1. TRANSFORMING RIT: THE CAMPAIGN FOR GREATNESS

Campaign Priorities

Pillar 1 Attract Exceptional Talent ($200 million goal)

Increase student quality and diversity through scholarships
Lead through faculty professorships
Grow student research fellowships

Pillar 2 Enhance the Student Experience ($280 million goal)

Broaden opportunities for experiential education
Build innovative maker and learning facilities
Strengthen the performing arts

Pillar 3 Improve the World through Research and Discovery ($400 million goal)

Promote interdisciplinary research centers
Expand fundamental research programs
Enhance applied and corporate research activities
Improve and expand research facilities

Pillar 4 Lead Future Special Initiatives ($120 million goal)

Build academic programs
Grow unrestricted and endowment support

Source: Transforming RIT: The Campaign for Greatness. https://www.rit.edu/transformingrit/ (accessed November 30, 2020).

improve the world through research and discovery (goal $400 million); and lead future initiatives (goal $120 million). The latter encompasses the broad purposes of support for academic programs, additions to unrestricted endowment, and unrestricted giving.

CAMPAIGN PLANNING AND STRATEGIES

Campaign planning had begun under President Destler with a comprehensive internal needs assessment that engaged all of the deans. As campaign planning evolved under President Munson, new interdisciplinary projects were identified and were incorporated as campaign priorities. Two early studies were undertaken to inform campaign planning, one conducted by the firm Bentz Whaley Flessner and another by consultants Brakeley Briscoe (Thrall, 2021).

At many universities, administrative offices operate in silos and do not always work closely together in planning. An unusual feature, and perhaps a central benefit, of planning RIT's blended campaign was that it required a close collaboration among three vice presidents—those for development and alumni relations; research; and government and community relations (Thrall, 2021).

THE BLENDED CAMPAIGN

The blended campaign strategy was unusual, although not unique. Northeastern University, in Boston, had launched such a campaign in 2013, with a $1 billion goal to be obtained equally from philanthropy and government sources. That goal was increased to $1.25 billion in 2015 and concluded in 2017, having raised $1.4 billion (St. Martin, 2017). RIT's campaign planners consulted with advancement leaders at Northeastern and found the model to be an attractive option (Thrall, 2021).

RIT's adoption of the blended campaign model was related to its own history and recent emergence as a Carnegie-classified research university (Joslyn, 2019). Entering into this new league was an achievement for RIT, but in order to increase its ranking among its new peers, it would need to expand its research. That dictated a strategic emphasis on partnerships with business and government as well as philanthropy directed to supporting research. And RIT's history suggested that securing research support through philanthropy might be especially daunting. At the same time, RIT needed to maintain its commitment to the undergraduate experience.

Speaking about the campaign while it was still in its quiet phase, then President Destler explained his view of the fundraising challenge. Despite tracing its origins to the nineteenth century, RIT had existed in current form only since the 1940s and its academic mission had evolved in recent decades. Indeed, many of its signature programs, such as the bachelor's degree in software engineering, had not been introduced until the 1990s. In the past, many of its students were employed at locally based companies, such as Xerox and

Kodak, and attended part time. Looking at the landscape in 2014, Destler observed, "Our older alums went to a very different kind of institution. A lot of those older alums went to classes at night and their companies may have paid for it, so they may have felt more loyalty to the companies for doing that" (Dougherty, 2014).

In this environment, Destler thought that philanthropy alone would be unlikely to produce the resources needed to advance RIT's research agenda and, indeed, that research might not be the highest priority for its alumni and existing donors. Perhaps the blended campaign strategy could provide donors with incentives to support research-related purposes by providing the opportunity to gain leverage and impact by joining with corporate, government, and other partners (Dougherty, 2014). The blended approach also could be a strategy to being more competitive for support from the State of New York, which often required matching with private funds (Thrall, 2021).

EXAMPLES OF THE BLENDED APPROACH

One example of the blended approach was a new building for RIT's new Magic Spell Studios, which relates to the creation of film, animation, and interactive games. The project blended government, corporate, and individual philanthropic support. Recognizing the potential economic impact, New York State committed $13.5 million, which was matched with corporate gifts from Cisco and Dell. When funding fell short, the difference was met through a $1.5 million gift from the Wegman Family Charitable Foundation, associated with the family of Danny Wegman, chairman of Rochester-based Wegmans Food Market. There was still a need for additional technology, so RIT allocated an additional $1 million from the $50 million gift from alumnus Austin McChord (Joslyn, 2019).

Another example is RIT's Global Cybersecurity Institute. In 2018, the State of New York provided a $5 million grant toward establishment of the Institute, with the expectation of three-to-one matching with private resources. Again, Austin McChord's gift provided $8 million toward the project, with the remaining $7 million needing to be secured from other individual and corporate donors (Rochester Institute of Technology, n.d.-e).

CAMPAIGN LEADERSHIP AND MANAGEMENT

The campaign is led by two co-chairs, Thomas F. Judson Jr. and Kevin J. Surace, both RIT alumni. Judson is located in the Rochester area and Surace in California, which has a growing concentration of RIT alumni. The board of trustees' development committee and deans' advisory councils receive updates on the campaign and some are engaged in interactions with donors. An on-campus campaign cabinet, comprised of deans and other officers, also monitors campaign progress (Thrall, 2021). But there is no volunteer structure specifically focused on the campaign.

The blended campaign strategy departed from previous campaigns and initially created some confusion regarding the crediting of non-philanthropic revenues. That required discussions to explain the campaign priorities in terms of partnerships that would include both faculty and advancement office initiatives. It also required particular emphasis on communication and transparency in campaign accounting and reporting (Thrall, 2021).

The blended approach made accounting and reporting more laborious than it would be in a traditional campaign—the buckets were not as simple as endowment, buildings, and annual giving. The research office and advancement office at RIT, as at most universities, use different standards for how they record and value revenues. Most advancement offices follow standard guidelines for crediting gifts and commitments toward a campaign goal, such as those recommended by the Council for Advancement and Support of Education. In the case of research support, such guidelines inform the distinction between grants, which are philanthropic in nature, and contracts, which are not. Few campaigns credit funds from government toward their campaign goals.

RIT's blended campaign definition sometimes led to ambiguous cases and questions that required discussion, for example, whether certain government grants should be credited to "research" or "government." That required considerable administrative time and effort throughout the campaign (Castleberry, 2021). Complicated accounting also required particular diligence to assure that reported totals were accurate and consistent with campaign crediting policies (Thrall, 2021).

CHALLENGES AND OPPORTUNITIES

Launching an unusual blended campaign for an institution that was in transition—in its academic classification as well as its leadership—required some nimble adjustments in campaign planning, communications, and management.

Planning through a Presidential Transition

The campaign was already in its quiet phase when President Munson succeeded President Destler in 2017. Knowing that the new president would want to add priorities to both the strategic plan and the campaign priorities, advancement leaders delayed the campaign announcement, although it already had achieved 60 percent of its $700 million preliminary goal. Some donors also held back on making their final decisions until the arrival of the new president and formal announcement of the campaign.

The addition of new priorities to a campaign that was already underway when the new president arrived also required some further redefinition of what comprised the four pillars that encompassed campaign priorities. That required further readjustments in campaign crediting policies, which, as discussed previously, were already complex due to the campaign's blended nature (Thrall, 2021).

Integrating a New Marketing Plan

Planning for Transforming RIT: The Campaign for Greatness also coincided with development of a new institution-wide marketing campaign, including a rebranding initiative. RIT had undertaken a marketing study in 2017 to evaluate awareness and perceptions of its quality relative to peers. That study informed the new marketing campaign, which was formally launched in 2019. The new institutional messages and visuals needed to be integrated into materials for the fundraising campaign that was already underway (Thrall, 2021).

Adapting to a Pandemic

Like all universities conducting campaigns in 2020, RIT was impacted by the Covid-19 pandemic. Phil Castleberry had been on the job as vice president for five weeks when much of the world shut down! But there was still an ongoing campaign that had not yet reached its goal.

Events, including board meetings, switched to a virtual format and saw substantially *increased* participation. But the impact on fundraising was mixed. Gift officers were able to close gifts that were already in the pipeline through virtual visits. Some were able to obtain virtual first visits with new prospective donors, but not all donors were receptive. The number of contacts with donors declined during 2020, before showing some encouraging increase in early 2021 (Thrall, 2021).

Looking beyond the pandemic in early 2021, Phil Castleberry envisioned a return to in-person donor visits once the pandemic had retreated. But there could be a continuing role for virtual visits as well. For example, gift officers meeting with a donor prospect in person might be able to add the president or a dean to the session using Zoom or another platform. That might actually increase the availability of those officers to donors, while using their time efficiently and reducing travel costs. Castleberry envisioned a post-Covid future of contacts with donors that might become, like RIT's campaign, "blended" in terms of the formats they would employ.

Given the impact of the pandemic and other considerations, a decision was reached in early 2021 to extend the closing date of the campaign from 2022 to 2023. A re-launch event was planned for fall, 2021, to include a re-emphasis on the philanthropic component of the campaign during its final two years (Castleberry, 2021).

LESSONS LEARNED AND LOOKING TO THE FUTURE

The blended campaign strategy was designed to fit a particular moment in RIT's history—its emergence as a doctoral university—and the goal of increasing its research activity, shared by two successive presidents. Its emphasis on partnerships and research, encompassing support from all sources, helped to accelerate its standing in the new league.

The blended campaign achieved its purpose of increasing support for research, marking RIT's emergence as a research university. In that regard, it was a success. But would RIT's next campaign follow the same approach? Castleberry sees RIT's continued advancement as requiring increased institutional resources, such as endowment, facilities, and funds for scholarship support. That would require a substantial increase in philanthropic giving, possibly leading to a more traditional strategy for the next comprehensive campaign.

Castleberry also notes that RIT's donor constituency and culture of philanthropy have evolved over the years of Transforming RIT: The Campaign for Greatness. While its early history did indeed include many part-time students, who may not have developed a strong affinity to the institution or acquired wealth in their careers, many RIT alumni of recent decades have become successful technology entrepreneurs. They are now located across the country, including Silicon Valley, Austin, Texas, and in other prospering urban centers. Castleberry mentions the example of Austin McChord, the $50 million donor, who has become a role model and mentor to RIT students seeking to follow in his footsteps (Castleberry, 2021).

By 2021, anticipating completion of Transforming RIT: The Campaign for Greatness in 2023, Castleberry and his team were already looking beyond it and preparing for the next campaign. That preparation would include expansion and reorganization of the advancement staff, aimed at putting more gift officers in the field, identifying more principal and major gift donors, and building a volunteer network to provide leadership for the next campaign—which likely would not be many years away (Castleberry, 2021).

REFERENCES

Castleberry, Phillip D. 2021. Interview with author, February 25, 2021.
"Celebrating 50 Years at the Henrietta Campus." 2018. *R.I.T: The University Magazine*, fall. https://www.rit.edu/sites/rit.edu/files/documents/research-magazines/Fall2018.pdf (accessed November 25, 2020).
Dougherty, Nate. 2014. "RIT Aims to Grow by Focusing on What Sets It Apart." *Rochester Business Journal*, November 28. https://rbj.net/2014/11/28/rit-aims-to-grow-by-focusing-on-what-sets-it-apart/ (accessed February 21, 2021).
Finnerty, Bob. 2006a. "Lisa Cauda Named RIT Vice President." Press release, July 17. https://www.rit.edu/news/lisa-cauda-named-rit-vice-president (accessed November 27, 2020).
Finnerty, Bob. 2006b. "Fundraising Campaign for RIT Tallies $309 Million." Press release, July 12. https://www.rit.edu/news/fundraising-campaign-rit-tallies-309-million (accessed December 8, 2020).
Finnerty, Bob. 2020a. "Phil Castleberry named Vice President for Development and Alumni Relations." Press release, January 8. https://www.rit.edu/news/phil-castleberry-named-vice-president-development-and-alumni-relations (accessed November 27, 2020).
Finnerty, Bob. 2020b. "Development and Alumni Relations is now University Advancement." Press release, October 6. https://www.rit.edu/news/development-and-alumni-relations-now-university-advancement (accessed November 30, 2020).
Goodman, James. 2017. "New RIT President to Build on the School's Strengths, With More Focus on Research and Arts." *Democrat & Chronicle*, June 8. https://www.democratandchronicle.com/story/news/2017/06/08/rit-research-colleges-universities-president-munson/379995001/ (accessed March 1, 2021).
Joslyn, Heather. 2019. "The Benefits of a Blended Campaign." *Chronicle of Philanthropy*, April 2. https://www.philanthropy.com/article/the-benefits-of-a-blended-campaign/ (accessed January 8, 2021).
Mozer, Mindy. 2016. "RIT Transitions to Top-tier University." Press release, November 16. https://www.rit.edu/news/rit-transitions-top-tier-university (accessed February 19, 2021).
"Powered by the Future." 2002. *RIT: The University Magazine*, winter, 6–10. https://www.rit.edu/sites/rit.edu/files/documents/research-magazines/Winter2002.pdf (accessed November 30, 2020).
"Rochester Institute of Technology 175th Anniversary: Funding the Future." 2004. *Rochester Business Journal*, May 14. https://rbj.net/2004/05/14/rochester-institute-of-technology-175th-anniversary-funding-the-future/ (accessed December 8, 2020).
Rochester Institute of Technology. n.d.-a. History of RIT. (Website) https://www.rit.edu/history-rit (accessed November 25, 2020).
Rochester Institute of Technology. n.d.-b. Co-op. (Website) https://www.rit.edu/cooperative-education (accessed November 25, 2020).
Rochester Institute of Technology. n.d.-c. National Technical Institute for the Deaf. (Website) https://www.rit.edu/ntid/about-ntid (accessed November 25, 2020).

Rochester Institute of Technology. n.d.-d. "Greatness Through Difference: The RIT Strategic Plan 2018-2025." https://www.rit.edu/strategicplan/documents/RIT-Strategic-Plan-Summary.pdf (accessed November 30, 2020).

Rochester Institute of Technology. n.d.-e. "Campaign Success." https://www.rit.edu/transformingrit/mission-statement (accessed January 14, 2021).

Rochester Institute of Technology. 2021. "University Advancement Focuses on Future." Press release, January 15. https://www.rit.edu/news/university-advancement-focuses-future (accessed February 25, 2021).

Rosen, Ellen. 2017. "Alumnus Gives RIT $50 Million to Foster Entrepreneurship and Cybersecurity." Press release, December 13. https://www.rit.edu/news/alumnus-gives-rit-50-million-foster-entrepreneurship-and-cybersecurity (accessed February 19, 2021).

Rosen, Ellen, Mindy Mozer, and Vienna McGrain. 2018. "RIT Publicly Launches $1 Billion Blended Campaign." Press release, July 13. https://www.rit.edu/news/rit-publicly-launches-1-billion-blended-campaign (accessed January 8, 2021).

St. Martin, Greg. 2017. "Northeastern Raises $1.4 billion, Shatters Empower Campaign Goal." Press release, October 27. https://news.northeastern.edu/2017/10/27/northeastern-raises-1-4-billion-shatters-empower-campaigns-goal/#:~:text=Northeastern%20University%20on%20Thursday%20night,students%2C%20faculty%2C%20and%20research.&text=Two%20years%20ago%2C%20due%20to,25%20percent%2C%20to%20%241.25%20billion. (accessed February 21, 2021).

Thrall, Eileen Galinski. 2021. Interview with author, February 17, 2021.

Chapter 3

Tulane University

ONLY THE AUDACIOUS: THE CAMPAIGN FOR AN EVER BOLDER TULANE

Tulane University, in New Orleans, Louisiana, traces its origins to the founding of the Medical College of Louisiana in 1834, which later became the University of Louisiana, a public institution. In 1884, a wealthy merchant, Paul Tulane, gave $1 million in land, cash, and securities "for the promotion and encouragement of intellectual, moral, and industrial education." The University of Louisiana was privatized and became Tulane University (Tulane University, 2021a). In 1886, the H. Sophie Newcomb Memorial College was established as Tulane's coordinate college for women. Today, Tulane is governed by the Board of Tulane, which is also known as the Board of Administrators of the Tulane Educational Fund.

Tulane is a doctoral university with the Carnegie classification of Research-1, signifying very high research activity. The university encompasses ten schools, including architecture, business, liberal arts, professional advancement, public health and tropical medicine, science and engineering, law, medicine, social work, and Newcomb-Tulane College, the undergraduate unit. Undergraduate programs are based on Tulane's main campus, called the uptown campus. A downtown campus houses the School of Medicine, School of Public Health and Tropical Medicine, and the School of Social Work, and is the main campus of the Tulane Medical Center. The Tulane University Hospital is a for-profit entity, owned jointly by the university and Hospital Corporation of America (Tulane University, 2021b).

Tulane has its own distinctive traditions, including the Hullabaloo cheer at athletic events and the Wave Goodbye party on the academic quad before commencement. Student life is strongly influenced by the features and culture of New Orleans, including the French Quarter, Mardi Gras, and the Creole cuisine (Tulane University, 2021c).

ADVANCEMENT AT TULANE

Ginny Wise was appointed as senior vice president of advancement in 2016, having served as Tulane's vice president of development for leadership giving since 2010. Wise had grown up in New Orleans as the daughter and granddaughter of Tulane alumni. She returned after graduating from Dartmouth College, earning a master's degree in education from Harvard, and serving in various advancement leadership positions at Harvard, including executive director of university development and associate dean of the Harvard Divinity School (Tulane University, 2016). Wise succeeded executive vice president for development and alumni relations Yvette Jones, who had served Tulane, in various positions, for 36 years and had directed the university's most recent campaign (Jasmin, 2017a).

Wise renamed the office of university relations and development as the office of advancement and completed a major re-organization, resulting in a centralized program. School-assigned gift officers work closely with the deans, but are centrally located and report ultimately to the senior vice president. Wise also significantly expanded the overall advancement staff, including regional gift officers and a dedicated principal gifts team, also reporting to the central advancement office (Hoffman, 2021). Campaign-related communications are managed by a team within the advancement office, in close coordination with the university office of communications and marketing.

SURVIVAL, RECOVERY, RENEWAL

On August 29, 2005, Hurricane Katrina hit New Orleans as the worst natural disaster in the nation's history to that time. More than 1,500 lives were lost, 80 percent of the region's population was displaced, and most of Tulane's uptown campus was covered in water. The damage to university buildings was extensive and made them uninhabitable. As then President Scott Cowen recalled, "By the time we finally evacuated to Houston, Texas, on the Friday after the storm, Tulane University no longer existed" (Cowen, 2007).

The Tulane administration made three bold decisions: to reopen by January 2006; to continue paying faculty and staff as long as possible; and to ask other institutions to take in displaced Tulane students until the campus could be reopened. The Tulane School of Medicine relocated students and essential faculty to Houston, Texas, and continued its fall semester at Baylor College of Medicine.

The 2006 target date for reopening was achieved, but the university faced projected ongoing budget deficits and its long-term survival would require difficult decisions. One that proved controversial was the closing of Newcomb College as a separate entity. Other recovery strategies included consolidating schools and units, reducing the number of doctoral programs, developing a new strategy for the medical school, and creating new partnerships in the community. The latter included making a service-learning course mandatory for all undergraduate students, with a focus on community development (Cowen, 2007).

PROMISE AND DISTINCTION

Tulane had launched the quiet phase of a campaign, "Promise and Distinction: The Campaign for Tulane," in 1999 and had announced it just months before Katrina struck. The campaign was suspended during the recovery, but was later restarted and by 2008 had raised more than $730 million, exceeding its $700 million goal (Schlueter, 2008). The campaign's success was announced by then President Cowen and campaign co-chair Cathy Pierson at the fall homecoming that year, the first since 2004 to include a Tulane football game played outdoors. Cowen identified the occasion as "a pivotal moment in the long and distinguished history of Tulane University [and] . . . a transformative time for our university, our city and state" (Schlueter, 2008).

Tulane was indeed ready to pivot—from survival, recovery, and renewal to a new era focused on crossing boundaries and raising sights.

CROSSING BOUNDARIES

In 2014, Scott Cowen retired from the Tulane presidency after 16 years. Despite the controversy that had accompanied some decisions in the recovery from Katrina, he left with considerable acclaim for his leadership during the crisis (Pope, 2014).

Michael A. Fitts, long-serving dean of the University of Pennsylvania law school and a distinguished legal scholar, was appointed as Tulane's fifteenth president. Fitts emphasized his commitment to "crossing boundaries." That would include fostering interdisciplinary academic work, increasing Tulane's impact on global problems, and strengthening the university's connections to New Orleans (Tulane University Office of the President, 2016). Fitts expanded on the connection between the university and city that had endured the trauma of Katrina together, saying "Tulane would not be the university it is without New Orleans and New Orleans is a more vibrant city with greater promise and potential than ever before because of Tulane" (Strecker, 2021).

Fitts created two planning committees, one focused on academic programs and another on diversity. Priorities identified through these efforts coincided with Fitts's emphasis on research and a cross-disciplinary approach. Some individual schools developed formal strategic plans, but given differences in readiness among the units—and recognition of the dynamic environment—Tulane did not adopt a formal strategic plan at the university-wide level (Wise, 2021).

Achieving the goals that Fitts envisioned would require substantially greater financial resources. He especially addressed the need for increased endowment, explaining that "For decades, we've accomplished spectacular, remarkable things with only a fraction of the endowment of some of our wealthier peers . . . I don't know about you, but I've had enough of running a marathon from 15 yards behind" (Jasmin, 2017b).

ONLY THE AUDACIOUS

With Michael Fitts's arrival in 2014, planning for a new campaign was already underway—counting had begun in 2011 (Lipinski, 2014a). But momentum was soon to accelerate, especially after the appointment of Ginny Wise in 2016.

CAMPAIGN PLANNING AND STRATEGIES

The university engaged the fundraising consulting firm of Marts & Lundy. The firm applied analytics to evaluate the giving capacity of Tulane's donor base, conducted a feasibility study, advised on restructuring of the advancement team, and provided ongoing counsel to the campaign.

One central strategy was an emphasis on campaign messaging and communication. A white paper summarizing suggested themes was developed and distributed to donors and other engaged constituents across the country. Focus groups were consulted to test reactions and gain advice, resulting in the definition of four pillars adopted for the campaign (Hoffman, 2021). The marketing firm 160over90 (https://www.160over90.com/) was engaged to help further develop the themes for the campaign and select a campaign tagline.

Ginny Wise identifies the extensive constituent engagement as a critical component of campaign planning. Given her deep roots with both New Orleans and Tulane, she felt the pulse of both. Katrina had devastated New Orleans, but indeed, the city had been in economic decline for many years before. Malaise remained and many were cautious. Given its close ties to the city, the university and its constituents had been affected by that history as well. Wise knew that a successful campaign would require more than executing established fundraising practices. It would be necessary to create a shift in culture and raise sights—on campus and among potential donors. As Wise describes it, New Orleans and Tulane needed to move beyond a mindset of "doing more with less" to one of "doing more with more" (Wise, 2021).

The tagline "only in New Orleans" had long been part of Tulane's enrollment marketing, communicating an attitude of uniqueness and pride. The name of the new campaign (Only the Audacious) and its tagline (encompassing the phrase "ever bolder Tulane") was intended to tap and rekindle that mindset, signaling that Tulane was prepared to move beyond survival and recovery to pursue bold goals. As Wise (2021) describes, the purpose was to give Tulane "the luxury to dream."

CAMPAIGN LEADERSHIP

Volunteer leadership for the campaign was organized at multiple levels. Four long-time Tulane supporters and trustees—Richard Yulman, Phyllis Taylor, and Catherine and Hunter Pierson—led an Executive Campaign Council (Strecker, 2017a). A National Campaign Council was created, co-chaired by David Mussafer, Ann Tenenbaum, and Thomas H. Lee. The national council encompassed regional committees across the country. In addition, some deans' councils would provide campaign leadership at the school level, focusing on unit priorities (Tulane University, 2019).

Ginny Wise (2021) identifies Tulane's approach to the regional campaign organization as distinctive. In many campaigns, regional committees operate relatively independently, which can make it difficult to establish consistency. Tulane's regional committees were connected under the umbrella of the National Campaign Council, to which regional chairs belong. That assured coordination of campaign activities and communications across the country.

THE BIG REVEAL

The campaign went public at a 2017 event called "The Big Reveal." The kick-off day included an afternoon celebration, announcement of the campaign by President Fitts, remarks by campaign volunteer leaders, and entertainment. That included a mock late-night talk show hosted by Tulane's provost, and a simulated NPR podcast called "Out to Lunch" at the famous New Orleans restaurant Commander's Palace (Morse, 2017). Activities beyond the formal event included a reception talk by Walter Isaacson, a noted historian and Tulane professor, and an after-party concert called the Tipping Point. That featured Grammy winners, Rock & Roll Hall of Fame inductees, and "New Orleans musical royalty" (160/90, n.d.). The day was particularly celebratory due to the unusual occurrence of snow!

The Big Reveal included announcement of a $1.3 billion goal, making Only the Audacious the largest campaign in Tulane's history. But the announcement did not include a formal end date for the campaign. Wise (2021) notes that the history of economic challenges and lingering post-Katrina uncertainty led some to remain cautious about Tulane's fundraising potential. As she explains, it was important to keep the message focused on Tulane's large ambitions rather than emphasizing a campaign timetable.

CAMPAIGN PRIORITIES

Campaign priorities for Only the Audacious were organized under four pillars, with specific objectives nested under each. As summarized in Table 3.1, the four pillars include pioneering research; transformative teaching; opportunity and diversity; and building an environment for excellence (Only the Audacious, n.d.).

Objectives identified under the pillars include funds dedicated to research; increasing the number of endowed faculty positions across the university and establishing more Presidential Chairs for distinguished faculty; more money for endowed scholarships; and various facilities projects. Projects highlighted at the time of the campaign's kickoff included construction of a new dining hall; new innovative spaces for medical students; combined space for programs dedicated to student success and careers; and expansion of the business school complex (Strecker, 2017a).

The campaign has specific goals for each of the objectives, including scholarships, endowed chairs, and facilities projects, and progress is tracked against those goals, rather than under the pillars. Schools and units also have specific campaign priorities, but no formal monetary goals (Hoffman, 2021). In addition to dollars, there is an explicit goal for doubling alumni engagement, from 25,000 to 50,000, during the period of the campaign (Strecker, 2018).

LEADERSHIP GIFTS

More than 54,000 commitments were made during the quiet phase of the campaign, totaling $820 million toward the $1.3 billion goal. That nucleus fund, announced at the kickoff, included substantial leadership gifts from

Table 3.1. Tulane University: Only the Audacious Campaign Priorities

Pillar	Objectives
Pioneering research	• Increase endowment dedicated to clinical and translational research. • Create an innovative fund to jump-start ideas and secure federal research funding. • Ensure all interested students can participate in research opportunities. • Create Presidential Chairs to attract high-profile multi-disciplinary faculty whose influence and mentorship will elevate the entire university.
Opportunity and diversity	• Dramatically increase the percentage of students from underrepresented communities. This funding [for financial aid] will close the financial gap and enable the best and the brightest to receive a Tulane education.
Transformative teaching	• Increase the number of endowed faculty positions across the university.
Building an environment that supports excellence	• The Commons • Yulman Stadium • Mussafer Hall, home to student services • Goldring/Woldenberg Business Complex • Paul Hall for Science and Engineering • Digital Scholarship Center, with focus on the humanities and sciences, as part of Howard-Tilton Memorial Library

Source: Strecker, Mike. 2018. "This Is Big." *Tulane Magazine*, March. https://issuu.com/tulaneuniversity/docs/tumag-mar2018 (accessed April 17, 2021).

some long-time Tulane donors, including four at the level of $10 million or more (Strecker, 2017a).

The Weatherhead Foundation, overseen by Tulane alumna and board member Celia Weatherhead and her husband Albert J. Weatherhead III, had committed $100 million. The gift would establish university-wide professorships and the Weatherhead Scholars Program, providing scholarships to students with high academic ability who are also dedicated to public service (Tulane University, 2011).

Dr. John Winton Deming had graduated from the Tulane Medical School and went on to practice internal medicine in Alexandria, Louisiana. He had maintained a lifelong relationship with the Tulane Medical Center as a faculty member, board member, and major donor until his passing in 1996. To honor his memory and dedication to Tulane, his widow, Bertie Deming Smith, gave $25 million to support research and name the John W. Deming Department of Medicine (Strecker, 2017b).

The Yulman family had been engaged with Tulane in multiple ways. Richard Yulman, the retired co-chairman and owner of mattress company Serta International, was a Tulane board member and campaign co-chair.

His daughter, Katy, was a co-chair of the National Campaign Council for the Tri-State area. The family had made a $20 million gift to name Tulane's football stadium, which opened in 2014 and became a symbol of the university's post-Katrina renaissance. The Yulmans made an additional $10 million commitment to Only the Audacious and designated $5 million as a challenge to match other gifts establishing endowed scholarship funds (Davis, 2021).

Directly addressing President Fitts's emphasis on a cross-disciplinary approach to education and fostering innovative approaches to social problems, the foundation associated with Tulane board member and alumnus Phyllis M. Taylor committed $15 million to create the Phyllis M. Taylor Center for Social Innovation and Design Thinking. The center would engage in teaching, research, and the practice of social innovation and design thinking, intended to advance a more just and equitable society (Lipinski, 2014b).

CHALLENGES AND OPPORTUNITIES

Ginny Wise and Christine Hoffman identify the key challenges faced in the campaign as the need to build the culture of philanthropy and the donor prospect pipeline; adapting to leadership changes in the university; and, of course, responding to the Covid-19 pandemic that began in 2020.

BUILDING THE CULTURE AND THE PIPELINE

Although Tulane had completed previous campaigns, there was not a strong culture of philanthropy. Sights were low and there was not a well-established pipeline of donor prospects. The culture was addressed through campaign marketing initiatives discussed previously, but new advancement management efforts also were required. Research was intensified in order to identify new prospective donors and build gift officer portfolios. There also was a need to increase the engagement of donors and prospects, addressed through expanding the reunion program and increasing the pace of personal visits by gift officers (Wise, 2021).

ADAPTING TO LEADERSHIP CHANGES

The quiet phase of the campaign had begun under president Scott Cowen, and the campaign needed to evolve in order to encompass priorities of the new administration of Michael Fitts. There also was substantial turnover among other administrative leaders during the campaign's early years, including the provost and deans.

Campaign director Christine Hoffman worked with deans in identifying their units' philanthropic priorities, but turnover required reimagining priorities for the schools. While that added some complications, there also was a bright side—new deans had been appointed with clear expectations as to their own fundraising roles and an understanding of the centralized advancement structure that Wise had implemented (Hoffman, 2021).

RESPONDING TO COVID-19

Similar to other universities, Tulane shifted many events and meetings to a virtual format and created new funds to raise money for students facing challenges. Covid required converting most donor contacts to virtual and it became difficult to initiate new relationships. However, increased electronic communication and solicitation proved highly effective at the leadership annual gifts level. Christine Hoffman predicts that such programs may be permanently changed, utilizing virtual and electronic methods and reducing costs over the traditional approach that relied on in-person visits (Hoffman, 2021).

Some observers speculated that Tulane's experience in responding to the disaster of Katrina may have honed its resilience and ability to improvise during the pandemic (Stewart, 2020). But, as Ginny Wise (2021) observes, the existential threat posed by Covid may also have rekindled the trauma of Katrina for some members of the New Orleans and Tulane communities, perhaps reinforcing lowered hopes that campaign messaging was working to overcome.

LESSONS LEARNED AND LOOKING TO THE FUTURE

By mid-2021, Wise was anticipating a successful conclusion to Only the Audacious, although no end date for the campaign had yet been announced. And she was beginning to focus on the long-run. Reflecting on the impact of the campaign on future Tulane fundraising, she noted that the university was ranked first among peer institutions in the number of new gifts at the $10,000 level. That indicates that the donor pipeline is growing, with positive implications for the future (Wise, 2021).

Will comprehensive campaigns be a part of the future—at Tulane and in higher education generally? Some people cite the growing sophistication of donors and their interest in the impact of their gifts as working against fundraising based on university-defined priorities. Wise (2021) acknowledges those points. But, she observes, campaigns also contribute to the visibility of philanthropy and help to build a giving culture. And, comprehensive campaigns that run over a period of years offer a wide range of institutional priorities, some of which are likely to coincide with those of many donors.

Reflecting on the impact of Only the Audacious on the university, coming just years after a disaster that threatened its existence, Wise returns to the themes embodied in the campaign's name and tagline—Tulane's unique strengths and boldness. The most important outcome of the campaign, she says, is that "Tulane grew up."

REFERENCES

160/90. n.d. Website. https://www.160over90.com/tulane (accessed April 30, 2021).

Cowen, Scott. 2007. "Tulane University: From Recovery to Renewal." *Liberal Education*, 93 (3), https://www.aacu.org/publications-research/periodicals/tulane-university-recovery-renewal (accessed April 16, 2021).

Davis, Patrick J. 2021. "Yulman Family Makes $5 Million Matching-challenge Gift to Expand Scholarships at Tulane." Press release, February 3. https://news.tulane.edu/pr/yulman-family-makes-5-million-matching-challenge-gift-expand-scholarships-tulane (accessed May 10, 2021).

Hoffman, Christine. 2021. Interview with author, April 26, 2021.

Jasmin, Alicia. 2017a. "Tulane Holds a Special Place for Yvette Jones." *Tulane News*, March 15. https://news.tulane.edu/news/tulane-holds-special-place-yvette-jones (accessed April 16, 2021).

Jasmin, Alicia. 2017b. "Tulane to Raise $1.3 Billion in 'Audacious' Campaign." *Tulane News*, December 8. https://news.tulane.edu/news/tulane-raise-13-billion-%E2%80%98audacious%E2%80%99-campaign (accessed April 17, 2021).

Lipinski, Jed. 2014a. "Tulane Prepares to Launch $1 Billion Fund-raising Campaign, President Michael Fitts Announces." *NOLA.com*, December 17. https://www.nola.com/news/education/article_365ac679-e95f-51cb-b4b1-f17d3c1f9630.html (accessed April 16, 2021).

Lipinski, Jed. 2014b. "Tulane Receives $15 Million Gift to Create Social Innovation Center." *NOLA.com*, November 18. https://www.nola.com/news/education/article_cc957018-361f-5ea2-9093-a83c45a5fa92.html (accessed May 10, 2021).

Morse, Paul. 2017. "Campaigning for Tulane." *Tulane News*, December 9. https://news.tulane.edu/news/campaigning-tulane (accessed April 17, 2021).

Only the Audacious. n.d. (Website) https://audacious.tulane.edu/ (accessed April 17, 2021).

Pope, John. 2014. "Scott Cowen Brought Tulane Back after Katrina, But Only After Conquering Uncertainty." *Times-Picayune*, June 13. https://www.nola.com/news/education/article_82b9af24-9890-5ef8-9aa8-5a7770d7898c.html (accessed April 16, 2021).

Schlueter, Carol J. 2008. "Coming Home to Celebrate Tulane's 'Pivotal Moment.'" *Tulane News*, October 1. https://news.tulane.edu/news/coming-home-celebrate-tulanes-pivotal-moment (accessed April 16, 2021).

Stewart, Mariah. 2020. "After Surviving Hurricane Katrina, Tulane University Is a Model for Recovering from Campus Closure." *Insight into Diversity*, May 18. https://www.insightintodiversity.com/after-surviving-hurricane-katrina-tulane-university-is-a-model-for-recovering-from-campus-closure/ (accessed April 16, 2021).

Strecker, Mike. 2017a. "Tulane University Launches Its Most Ambitious Fundraising Campaign with $1.3 Billion Goal." *Tulane News*, December 8. https://news.tulane.edu/pr/tulane-university-launches-its-most-ambitious-fundraising-campaign-13-billion-goal (April 17, 2021).

Strecker, Mike. 2017b. "$25 Million Gift Will Name John W. Deming Department of Medicine at Tulane University." Press release, September 18. https://news.tulane.edu/news/25-million-gift-will-name-john-w-deming-department-medicine-tulane-university (accessed May 10, 2021).

Strecker, Mike. 2018. "This Is Big." *Tulane Magazine*, March. https://issuu.com/tulaneuniversity/docs/tumag-mar2018 (accessed April 17, 2021).

Strecker, Mike. 2021. "Come Together." *Tulanian*, Spring. https://tulanian.tulane.edu/spring-2021/come-together (accessed April 17, 2021).

Tulane University. 2011. "Weatherhead Foundation Pledges Additional $50 Million to Tulane University." Press release, June 24. https://www.newswise.com/articles/weatherhead-foundation-pledges-additional-50-million-to-tulane-university (accessed May 10, 2021).

Tulane University. 2016. "Ginny Wise Named as Advancement Senior Vice President. Press release, December 1. https://news.tulane.edu/news/ginny-wise-named-advancement-senior-vice-president (accessed April 16, 2021).

Tulane University. 2019. *2018 Report on Philanthropy*. https://issuu.com/tulaneuniversity/docs/1550_cam_fy19_annual_report-issuu (accessed April 17, 2021).

Tulane University. 2021a. *History and Traditions*. https://tulane.edu/about/history-and-traditions (accessed April 16, 2021).

Tulane University. 2021b. *Schools and College*. https://tulane.edu/academics/schools-and-college (accessed April 16, 2021).

Tulane University. 2021c. *Life at Tulane*. https://tulane.edu/life-tulane (accessed April 16, 2021).

Tulane University Office of the President. 2016. *Speeches/Inauguration*. https://president.tulane.edu/inauguration-0 (accessed April 16, 2021).

Wise, Ginny. 2021. Interview with author, May 11, 2021.

Chapter 4

University of Virginia

HONOR THE FUTURE: THE CAMPAIGN FOR THE UNIVERSITY OF VIRGINIA

Founded by Thomas Jefferson in 1819, the University of Virginia (UVA) is a public university classified as Research-1, reflecting very high research activity. UVA's main campus is in Charlottesville, Virginia, the location of twelve schools and the medical center. The university was ranked as the fourth best public university by *U.S. News & World Report* in 2020 and its hospital was ranked as the best in Virginia in 2020–21 (University of Virginia, 2020a). In 1954, UVA established the College at Wise, which operates as a four-year liberal arts college, located in Southwest Virginia.

In addition to writing the Declaration of Independence and serving as the third president of the United States, Jefferson was an accomplished architect. He designed his home, known as Monticello, and his ideal "Academical Village," which remains the heart of the UVA campus. At the center of the Academical Village is "the Lawn," which is the scene of many events and includes a limited number of residential units. The focal point of the Academical Village is the Rotunda, designed by Jefferson and modeled on the Pantheon, a second-century temple in Rome.

UVA has its own distinction culture—and lingo—developed over the centuries since its founding. For example, students compete based on academic performance and service to be selected for a residential room on the Lawn and to thus be known as "Lawnies." At UVA, being on campus is described as being "on Grounds." One of the university's most distinctive traditions is its honor system. The system is administered by students and requires honorable behavior in all aspects of student life. Students who are found guilty of a violation by a jury of their peers are subject to permanent expulsion (University of Virginia, 2020b).

ADVANCEMENT AT UVA

UVA's organization for institutional advancement follows a hybrid model, including centralized and decentralized components. Advancement operations, communications, and planned giving are centralized services provided across the university. Advancement staff serving some schools and units have a dual reporting line into the central university advancement office, while other unit-based teams report to deans or unit heads. The health system development office coordinates fundraising for the hospital and the schools of medicine and nursing. As discussed later in this study, the development organization was historically more decentralized and evolved into a hybrid structure in anticipation of the Honor the Future campaign.

A distinctive feature of fundraising at UVA is the existence of multiple independent foundations, known as "University-affiliated organizations," which raise funds for their respective schools/units. Each foundation is a separate 501(c)(3) organization with its own leadership board (University of Virginia, 2020c).

The university has seen unusual continuity in its advancement leadership. Robert D. ("Bob") Sweeney served as vice president for more than 25 years, directing two campaigns raising more than $5 billion. Upon Sweeney's retirement in 2016, then university president Teresa Sullivan appointed Mark M. Luellen as vice president for advancement. Luellen had joined UVA in 2014 as senior associate vice president for development, working with Sweeney and leading the planning for a new campaign. Before joining UVA, he had led the advancement organization at the Pennsylvania State University College of the Liberal Arts (de Bruyn, 2016).

A LONG HISTORY OF CAMPAIGNS

The University of Virginia has a long history of undertaking organized campaigns. Based on his research in the UVA archives, Donald Hasseltine identified the first such effort as the Centennial Campaign, launched in 1917 with the goal of raising $3 million. Although comprehensive campaigns were not the norm in higher education in that era, the Centennial Campaign included goals for endowment, facilities projects, and other purposes. The campaign raised $1.3 million, but "stalled well short of its intended goal" (Hasseltine, 2002).

Fortunately, subsequent decades brought larger campaign goals and greater success. In 2000, under President John T. Casteen III and Vice President Bob

Sweeney, the university completed a campaign raising $1.43 billion, at the time the largest total in history for a public university (de Bruyn, 2016).

In 2006, Casteen announced a new campaign, The Campaign for the University of Virginia, with a goal of $3 billion, to be achieved by 2011. The campaign was comprehensive and included goals and priorities for all UVA schools and units. But the Great Recession that began in 2008 was an unanticipated setback. By the original deadline, UVA's campaign was still $400 million short of its goal. President Teresa Sullivan, who had become president in 2010, extended the campaign by two years. Bob Sweeney said that the goal had perhaps been too ambitious, but many universities in that period also faced a similar situation and extended their campaigns (Kiley, 2012).

The $3 billion goal was exceeded by the new deadline, in 2013, including gifts from more than 220,000 donors. Gifts had established more than 1,000 new endowed funds and supported various facilities projects ("Successful $3 Billion Campaign Propels U. Va. Forward," 2013). Among its largest gifts was a commitment of $100 million, to establish the Frank Batten School of Public Leadership and Public Policy (de Bruyn, 2016). But there was little time for reflection and celebration; planning for the next phase in the university's advancement began immediately.

A GREAT AND GOOD UNIVERSITY: THE 2030 PLAN

James E. Ryan was appointed as the ninth president of the University of Virginia in 2018, just a year before the institution's 200th anniversary. Ryan was dean of the Harvard Graduate School of Education and previously had served at UVA as the Matheson & Morgenthau Distinguished Professor of Law.

Within two months of taking office, Ryan appointed a strategic planning committee to define UVA's directions to the year 2030 (University of Virginia, 2019). The plan was developed through a participative process, with a planning committee comprised of faculty and administrators, which held over 100 outreach sessions with members of the university community. The 2030 Plan was presented to UVA's governing board, the Board of Visitors, in June 2019.

The plan retained the mission and values stated in the existing 2013 strategic plan, but set new goals for 2030. The university plan anticipated that individual schools and units would develop specific plans consistent with the 2030 plan's overarching goals:

- Strengthen our foundation, which includes supporting students, faculty, and staff.

- Cultivate the most vibrant community in higher education in order to prepare students to be servant leaders in a diverse and globally connected world.
- Enable discoveries that enrich and improve lives.
- Make UVA synonymous with service. (University of Virginia, 2019)

The plan articulated various sub-goals under each of the broad themes and identified ten key initiatives, some of which addressed multiple goals (University of Virginia, 2019). Although the plan anticipated various sources of revenue for its implementation, a campaign would be a critical strategy in achieving its vision for UVA's future (Luellen, 2021).

HONOR THE FUTURE

In October 2019, President Ryan announced UVA's new campaign, Honor the Future, with the goal of raising $5 billion by 2025. The kickoff included panel discussions with various prominent participants, an address by President Ryan, and a concert on the Lawn by famed singer Tony Bennett, who was joined on stage by UVA's popular basketball coach, also named Tony Bennett (Newman, 2019).

The campaign already had secured $2.75 billion toward its goal. Lead gifts included a gift of $120 million from a foundation associated with alumni Jaffray and Merrill Woodriff, toward establishment of a new school of data sciences (Hester, 2019), and a gift of $100 million from Jane and David Walentas, to establish a new scholarship program for first-generation students (Newman, 2019).

The kickoff event generated excitement and visibility. But the campaign had begun long before—and its formal announcement was not exactly a surprise. Planning had begun in 2014 following conclusion of the previous campaign and all gifts from that time forward would count toward the new campaign (McCance, 2018). In effect, UVA's campaigning had become continuous, or perpetual, with no gap between initiatives.

In 2018, departing from the traditional practice of not announcing a campaign until the quiet (or "silent") phase has been completed, UVA made public the fact that it was planning a new campaign, that the goal would be $5 billion, and that it would be *formally announced* a year later, in the fall of 2019, in connection with the university's bicentennial (McCance, 2018).

The rationale for both decisions—continuous counting and an early pre-announcement—was to maintain momentum and transparency in a period spanning a presidential transition. The strategy was endorsed by President Sullivan, although decisions were not finalized and the public announcement was deferred until President Ryan arrived in 2018 and concurred with the decision (Luellen, 2021).

One observer identifies UVA's early announcement as part of a trend, noting that with the silent phase of many campaigns running for four years, "they are only sort of silent" ("A Not-So-Silent Silent Phase," 2018). Another commentator suggested that earlier announcements might help to keep the institutional brand more visible and maintain excitement. However, others noted risks, including the inability to adjust the goal before it becomes public and the challenge of keeping donors interested over a long period of years ("A Not-So-Silent Silent Phase," 2018).

CAMPAIGN PRIORITIES

As shown in Table 4.1, priorities for Honor the Future were identified under three broad pillars—*community*, *discovery*, and *service*—consistent with the three overarching goals of the 2030 strategic plan. Each priority encompasses specific goals and provides examples of the purposes for which funds are to

Table 4.1. University of Virginia: Honor the Future Campaign Priorities

Community	Discovery	Service
1 Attract and support exceptionally talented students regardless of economic circumstances. a. Scholarships b. Advising	1 Recruit and retain excellent faculty committed to both teaching and research. a. Endowed chairs b. Teaching Excellence Fund	1 Make UVA the leading place in the country to study, teach, and sustain democracy. a. UVA Democracy Institute
2 Cultivate the best student experience in higher education. a. Leadership & Opportunity Fund b. Student well-being c. Arts and athletics	2 Enable discoveries that enrich and improve lives. a. Interdisciplinary facilities b. Grand Challenges Fund	2 Prepare students for lives of public service. a. Public service programs b. Loan forgiveness
3 Develop outstanding residential communities. a. Second-year housing b. Residential programming	3 Develop open grounds at EMMET/IVY. a. Design and build EMMET/IVY b. Access and programming	3 Be a good neighbor to Charlottesville and surrounding communities a. Community engagement b. Sustainability c. Access to quality healthcare

Source: Honor the Future Campaign Priorities. https://giving.virginia.edu/sites/default/files/2020-02/Campaign-Priorities-Slide_0.pdf (accessed November 23, 2020).

be raised. For example, the community priority includes attracting and supporting exceptionally talented and diverse students regardless of economic circumstances, which requires funds for scholarships and expanded advising.

Individual schools and units have their own specific priorities and goals. For example, the Darden School of Business, with a goal of $400 million, emphasizes support for new endowed faculty positions and funds for research; scholarships and the student experience; and specific technology and facilities projects (Powered by Purpose, 2020).

The Law School, also with a $400 million goal, identifies four priorities: scholarships and loan forgiveness; professorships; program and curricular initiatives; and unrestricted gifts (Wood, 2019). UVAHealth, including the School of Medicine, School of Nursing, and the Health System, set a goal of $1 billion, which emphasizes medical and nursing education and research and identifies major priorities by medical service lines, including cancer, brain sciences, transplant medicine, children's health, and precision medicine (UVAHealth, n.d.).

The School of Engineering, with a $250 million goal, identifies its "causes" as technology and innovation, faculty excellence, and the student experience (University of Virginia Office of Advancement, 2020). The campaign also includes a goal of $500 for UVA athletics, emphasizing athletic facilities and scholarships (White, 2019).

The campaign does not include specific non-monetary goals, such as alumni participation and engagement. Although the university considers participation to be important, the emphasis in the campaign is on principal and major gifts. As Mark Luellen explains, "While all gifts are important, universities can't rely only on participation rates, and our fundraising must be focused on top-line growth in overall commitments, which requires an emphasis on principal and major gifts" (Luellen, 2021).

CAMPAIGN PLANNING AND STRATEGIES

As mentioned previously, planning for Honor the Future began in 2014, immediately following the completion of the previous campaign. That campaign had been driven by dollar goals more than institutional priorities and the advancement leadership wanted to tie the new campaign more closely to institutional strategic objectives (Luellen, 2021). But a presidential transition was on the horizon and the 2030 plan had yet to be developed. It was impossible to know what university-wide priorities ultimately might emerge.

Planning through a Presidential Transition

Luellen was leading the campaign planning and determined that the circumstances required beginning with individual schools and units. Their priorities would be set by the deans, directors, and others at the unit level and were likely to remain relatively consistent, perhaps with some fine-tuning to coordinate with priorities of the new president and university strategic plan. Central advancement worked directly with the deans to identify and refine their fundraising priorities while awaiting the new president's arrival and the clarification of university-wide themes (Luellen, 2021).

Assessing and Refining the Model

The consulting firm of Grenzebach Glier and Associates (GG+A) was retained to undertake a comprehensive review of UVA's advancement program and operations in order to inform preparation for the new campaign. GG+A's report noted areas for improvement in UVA's fundraising program, emphasized the importance of sufficient funding to support a campaign, and urged a focus on attaining top-line growth in gift revenue (Luellen, 2021).

In order to assure sufficient budgetary support for the campaign, a new funding model was developed, in which costs would be shared between schools/units and central advancement. In addition, the Board of Visitors, UVA's governing board, authorized the vice president for advancement to leverage an administrative fee on the endowment to make strategic investments, up to certain limits. The sharing of expenses gave the schools and units a tangible stake in the campaign and potential access to endowment funds added greater flexibility (Luellen, 2021).

Restructuring Advancement Management

Preparation for the campaign also included restructuring of advancement management. As mentioned previously, UVA advancement historically had been highly decentralized, with many development staff reporting to deans and unit heads, with central advancement having only a coordinating role. Moving to a more centralized reporting model was essential in preparing for the campaign and also to gain the efficiency and effectiveness of a more structured approach.

Following extensive and collaborative discussions, memoranda of understanding were developed between central advancement and various deans and unit heads, providing for central direction of school development programs and staff. The result was a hybrid model. Some units remain relatively independent, but a number of the schools and units have entered closer relationships with central advancement and the trend has continued as the campaign has made the advantages of that approach more evident (Luellen, 2021).

Luellen notes some irony in the move from a decentralized to a hybrid structure under his leadership. "Before I came to UVA, I was a school-based development officer who often grappled with my university's central advancement office. I mentioned that to Bob Sweeney when he interviewed me and asked if he was sure I would be the right choice for a central role at UVA. Bob responded that he was well aware of my background and that he thought change might best be accomplished by 'bringing a fox into the henhouse'" (Luellen, 2021).

Donor Strategies

UVA's campaign reflects a donor-centered approach. Observing that contemporary donors desire both transparency and impact, Luellen explains that "Relationships with donors are becoming more like a concierge service than a traditional sales model" (Luellen, 2021). "We have donors who are fiercely loyal to the university and incredibly generous. But one thing that's different now is that instead of saying, 'Give what you can to this general project,' we are instead talking to them about, 'What are your philanthropic passions?' If they have a deep passion around research and autism, or they want to increase the study of English literature, these are goals that the university can help further and achieve" (Hayes, 2019).

Donors also have responded favorably to an innovative program of matching funds from the university for gifts supporting endowed scholarships and professorships, an approach that Luellen describes as "co-investment" by the university and donors (Luellen, 2021). For example, the University provided $40 million in matching funds to a gift of $100 million from David and Jane Walentas, which created a scholarship fund for first-generation students through the Jefferson Scholars Foundation, thus increasing the fund's impact (Hayes, 2019).

Luellen says, "[The matching funds approach] has been a game changer and really a new part of this campaign. People have [said], 'If this is a priority for the university and you're going to co-invest, then we're also going to invest and we're going to do this together'" (Hayes, 2019).

CAMPAIGN LEADERSHIP AND MANAGEMENT

The campaign is led by a volunteer executive committee of 35 individuals, with Peter Grant II as the chair and Martha Lubin Karsh and Malcolm

Brogdon serving as co-chairs. The chair is actively engaged in the day-to-day strategic efforts of the campaign, including solicitations, but the larger committee functions primarily in an advisory role. While most committee members are major donors, giving is not emphasized as the committee's primary responsibility.

The previous campaign had included an extensive regional structure, but it proved to be too large and unwieldy to manage. A survey of regional volunteers following the previous campaign suggested that it had evolved into more of a donor-recognition society, with major donors listed as members, but without any active role in the campaign and little sense of satisfaction from their role. Some UVA schools have established smaller regional committees for their component campaigns, but there is not a regional volunteer structure at the university level in the Honor the Future campaign (Luellen, 2021).

CHALLENGES AND OPPORTUNITIES

By the beginning of 2021, with four years still to go, Luellen was confident that the campaign goal would be achieved. New principal gifts continued to be announced, including a $50 million gift from Martha and Bruce Karsh to establish the Karsh Institute of Democracy at UVA, announced in June 2021. The gift would be part of a $100 million investment that UVA would make in the new institute (Newman, 2021).

But, like all campaigns underway in 2020 and continuing into 2021, UVA's efforts were impacted by the Covid-19 pandemic. The impact brought both challenges and opportunities. The comprehensive campaign model afforded opportunities to pivot and adapt to the circumstances in a way that more focused campaigns might be unable to accomplish.

Reordering Priorities

As Luellen explains, university strategic plans extend over a long period of time, so there is flexibility to emphasize some priorities over others in the short term. UVA gift officers maintained their contact with donors throughout the pandemic, emphasizing immediate needs, such as expendable scholarship support. Some donors were agreeable to shifting their support to those areas, even if they had not traditionally been their primary interest (Elucian, 2020).

The pivot did require conversations across the campus and decisions about priorities that needed to be deferred, at least temporarily. Luellen acknowledges that some of those conversations were "tough," but they were essential to respond to the focus of donors on more urgent needs (Elucian, 2020).

Shifting to the Virtual World

Along with challenges and the need for some difficult decisions, the pandemic also presented new opportunities. Virtual alumni events attracted more participants than in-person events in previous years, with participation up by 185 percent in 2020. Virtual events included alumni from a wider geographic range than in-person events could achieve, attracting alumni from more than 50 nations (Luellen, 2021).

Gift officers also increased virtual contacts with prospects and donors, and many support staff shifted to working off-campus. Luellen believes that the latter change will be permanent, making it possible to recruit individuals from outside of the Charlottesville area and increase the diversity of the advancement staff in the future. Most gift processing was out-sourced to a commercial firm, which also reduced the number of staff required to be working on campus (Luellen, 2021).

LESSONS LEARNED AND LOOKING TO THE FUTURE

The onset of the Covid-19 pandemic was a historic turning point. What does UVA's experience suggest about the lasting impact on campaign fundraising? Although some travel is certain to return after the pandemic, Luellen envisions the continued use of virtual contacts and events. As he observes, "Many donors prefer more structured and organized engagement and may be less open to the old 'Let's have a cup of coffee' approach" (Luellen, 2021).

Luellen also foresees a continued and growing emphasis on the use of data to identify donor interests and tailor messaging. "We don't want to be Big Brother," he explains. "We don't want to be creepy about the work that we're doing, but I think the data does give us the opportunity of using technology to better understand what people's interests and passions are" (Elucian, 2020). He also predicts that data will play an increasing role in setting campaign strategy, "using the data to discuss strategy and taking a moment of pause to think about it before getting sucked into the weeds of the next event. Logistics are important . . . but the strategy is even far more critical" (Elucian, 2020).

And what about the future of comprehensive campaigns? "We're in a perpetual fundraising mode now and going forward," Luellen observes, "and the challenge will be to maintain momentum and excitement" (Luellen, 2021). He speculates that campaigns may become essentially marketing umbrellas covering multi-year periods of an institution's ongoing fundraising, with new priorities and projects being introduced periodically throughout that long run. Comprehensive campaigns may come to encompass more mini-campaigns that are introduced and completed under their multi-year umbrellas, helping to maintain interest and generate excitement.

While metrics are important and the emphasis on data as a guide to strategy is likely to grow, Luellen emphasizes the need to remain focused on relationships, even as campaigns come to rely on more sophisticated technology. He observes that some development professionals have become focused on technical skills and easier-to-evaluate metrics, such as contacts and open rates on digital communications. Turnover in development positions is high and undermines the continuity of relationships. Some presidents are coming into their positions with little fundraising experience and stay for relatively brief tenures. These realities present challenges for the future.

In Luellen's view, UVA's success demonstrates that successful campaigns require focusing on top-line growth in gift commitments and an emphasis on principal and major gifts. Those gifts require maintaining and nourishing relationships with donors over the long run. How to do that in light of current patterns and realities is a challenge that advancement leaders will need to address in the years ahead (Luellen, 2021).

REFERENCES

"A Not-So-Silent Silent Phase." 2018. *Inside Higher Education*, July 6. https://www.insidehighered.com/news/2018/07/06/uvas-latest-fund-raiser-marks-new-trend-early-public-announcements (accessed November 23, 2020).

de Bruyn, Anthony P. 2016. "UVA Appoints Mark M. Luellen As Vice President for Advancement." *UVA Today*, June 6. https://news.virginia.edu/content/uva-appoints-mark-m-luellen-vice-president-advancement (accessed November 19, 2020).

Elucian. 2020. "How Philanthropy Can Amplify Outcomes for Higher Education: A Q&A with University of Virginia's VP for Advancement." https://www.ellucian.com/insights/how-philanthropy-can-amplify-outcomes-higher-education (accessed January 15, 2021).

Hasseltine, Donald. 2002. "Lessons for the Modern Campaign from the University of Virginia." *CASE International Journal of Educational Advancement* (4) 1, July 24, pp. 7–18.

Hayes, Heather B. 2019. "U. Va. Goes Big with $5 Billion Capital Campaign." *Virginia Business*, December 2. https://www.virginiabusiness.com/article/u-va-goes-big-with-5-billion-capital-campaign/ (accessed January 14, 2021).

Hester, Wesley P. 2019. "UVA Plans New School of Data Science; $120 Million Gift is Largest in University History." Press release, January 18. https://news.virginia.edu/content/uva-plans-new-school-data-science-120-million-gift-largest-university-history (accessed February 6, 2021).

Kiley, Kevin. 2012. "Oversized Check From Reality." *Inside Higher Education*, January 5. https://www.insidehighered.com/news/2012/01/05/university-virginia-falls-short-3-billion-fund-raising-goal (accessed November 20, 2020).

Luellen, Mark M. 2021. Interview with author, January 28, 2021.

McCance, McGregor. 2018. "UVA Announces Plans For $5 Billion Campaign." *UVA Today*, June 7. https://news.virginia.edu/content/uva-announces-plans-5-billion-campaign (accessed November 23, 2020).

Newman, Caroline. 2019. "Honor the Future: Campaign Kickoff Brings Fanfare, Reflection and Big Dreams." *UVA Today*, October 12. https://news.virginia.edu/content/honor-future-campaign-kickoff-brings-fanfare-reflection-and-big-dreams (accessed November 24, 2020).

Newman, Caroline. 2021. "Led by Karsh Family Gift, UVA Plans $100 Million for Institute of Democracy." Press release, June 4. https://news.virginia.edu/content/led-karsh-family-gift-uva-plans-100-million-institute-democracy (accessed July 7, 2021).

Powered by Purpose: The Darden Campaign in Support of Honor the Future. 2020. (Website) http://giving.darden.virginia.edu/ (accessed November 23, 2020).

"Successful $3 Billion Campaign Propels U. Va. Forward." 2013. *UVA Today*, May 19. https://news.virginia.edu/content/successful-3-billion-campaign-propels-uva-forward (accessed November 24, 2020).

University of Virginia. 2019. *A Great and Good University: The 2030 Plan*. Charlottesville, VA: author.

University of Virginia. 2020a. *Facts and Figures*. https://www.virginia.edu/facts (accessed November 19, 2020).

University of Virginia. 2020b. *Students and Traditions*. https://odos.virginia.edu/students-traditions (accessed November 19, 2020).

University of Virginia. 2020c. *Faculty Handbook: The Office of University Advancement*. https://provost.virginia.edu/faculty-handbook/office-university-advancement-0 (accessed November 19, 2020).

University of Virginia Office of Advancement. 2020. *Causes*. (Website) https://engineering.virginia.edu/advancement/causes (accessed November 24, 2020).

UVAHealth. n.d. Giving. (Website) https://giving.uvahealth.com/campaign (accessed November 23, 2020).

White, Jeff. 2019. "UVA Athletics Announces Campaign Goal." Press release, October 24. https://virginiasports.com/news/2019/10/24/jeff-white-master-plan/ (accessed November 23, 2020).

Wood, Mary. 2019. "UVA Law Launches 'Honor the Future' Capital Campaign." Press release, October 7. https://www.law.virginia.edu/news/201910/uva-law-launches-honor-future-capital-campaign (accessed November 23, 2020).

PART II

Master's Colleges and Universities

Master's Colleges and Universities in the Carnegie Classification of Institutions of Higher Education are institutions that offer at least fifty master's degrees. They do not meet the definition of research universities in terms of their awarding of doctoral degrees or research expenditures, although they may offer some doctoral degrees and undertake research. They are identified in three categories: Larger Programs (M1), Medium Programs (M2), and Smaller Programs (M3), based on the number of master's degrees awarded. These institutions were previously identified as "comprehensive universities and colleges," a term that some still use, although it is no longer a part of the Carnegie framework.

Master's colleges and universities generally have a regional focus and offer career-oriented graduate degrees. Some are private, but many are public institutions that had their origins as state colleges established to train teachers, also known as "normal schools." Some are facing financial pressures as a result of limited state funding, increased competition, and declining enrollments (Skipper, 2021).

They also face some challenges in fundraising. Most students do not come from backgrounds that include wealth or philanthropy and they do not attract substantial support from corporations and foundations that are primarily interested in research. However, facing pressure on other forms of support, some have successfully launched comprehensive campaigns, as demonstrated by the two cases discussed in this section: California State University, Los Angeles (Cal State LA) and Youngstown State University (YSU).

CALIFORNIA STATE UNIVERSITY, LOS ANGELES

Cal State LA is an urban university in Los Angeles that is designated as a Hispanic-Serving Institution, Minority-Serving Institution, and Asian American and Native American Pacific Islander-Serving Institution. It is ranked among top universities in terms of the upward social mobility of its graduates and emphasizes that goal and its impact on the Los Angeles community. Cal State LA had a modest fundraising program and had never conducted a campaign prior to arrival of its new president, William A. Covino, in 2013. Covino initiated a strategic planning process and, in 2018, launched the university's first campaign, We Are LA: The Campaign for Cal State LA, with a goal of $75 million. Despite a lack of fundraising history and well-established donor relationships, the campaign attracted principal gifts and by 2021 had exceeded its goal with $83 million in commitments. Despite this early success, the university made a strategic decision to continue the campaign to its planned closing date in 2022, while retaining the original goal.

YOUNGSTOWN STATE UNIVERSITY (YSU)

Youngstown State University (YSU) is located in a region of Ohio that has seen economic decline since the collapse of the steel industry in the 1970s. The state had identified the university as its best engine for economic resurgence, but YSU continued to struggle for enrollment and revenue, amidst turnover in its leadership. In 2014, the university's board selected James Tressel as the new president. Tressel was a local hero but an unconventional choice—the former coach of championship-winning football teams at YSU and Ohio State. He was committed to reversing the university's decline and increasing its impact on the region. In 2017, YSU announced "We See Tomorrow," a $100 million campaign focused on those goals. By 2020, a year ahead of schedule, the original goal had been exceeded and was increased to $125 million. That larger goal was exceeded by the original campaign closing date in 2021.

REFERENCE

Skipper, Eric. 2021. "The Plight and Promise of Regional Colleges and Universities." *Inside Higher Ed*, May 24. https://www.insidehighered.com/views/2021/05/24/recommendations-how-regional-colleges-can-survive-and-thrive-future-opinion (accessed May 24, 2021).

Chapter 5

California State University, Los Angeles

WE ARE LA: THE CAMPAIGN FOR CAL STATE LA

California State University, Los Angeles (Cal State LA) is a public university, one of 23 campuses that comprise the California State University (CSU) system. Governed by a board of trustees, CSU is the largest public university system in the nation, enrolling almost 500,000 students. Cal State LA enrolls about 26,000 students and is listed among Master's Colleges and Universities: Larger Programs (M1) in the Carnegie Classification framework (Cal State LA, 2021a).

Located in the heart of Los Angeles, the Cal State LA campus is on the site of one of California's 36 original adobes, built in 1709 by Franciscan missionaries on lands historically known as Rancho Rosa Castilla, once owned by rancher Juan Batista Batz. It was opened as Los Angeles State College in 1947, was renamed California State College at Los Angeles in 1964, and became Cal State LA in 1972 (Cal State LA, 2021a).

The university includes nine colleges, including arts and letters; business and economics; education; engineering, computer science, and technology; ethnic studies; natural and social sciences; professional and global education; the Honors College; and the Rongxiang Xu College of Health and Human Services, which includes the Patricia A. Chin School of Nursing (Cal State LA, 2021b).

In 2020, *U.S. News & World Report* ranked Cal State LA ninth among public regional universities in the western United States. Its program in engineering and computer science was ranked fifth in the nation among master's institutions and its business program ranked in the top ten among public universities in California (Cal State LA, 2020).

Cal State LA is a federally designated Hispanic-Serving Institution, Minority-Serving Institution, and Asian American and Native American

Pacific Islander-Serving Institution. Its students are about 51 percent Hispanic, 23 percent Asian American/Pacific Islander, 16 percent white, and 10 percent Black. In one study, it was ranked number one in the nation for the upward social mobility of its students (Cal State LA, 2021c). It is an anchor institution in the Coalition of Urban and Metropolitan Universities, which promotes the involvement of universities in transforming local economies and the social well-being of communities (Cal State LA, 2018).

ADVANCEMENT AT CAL STATE LA

Janet Schellhase Dial was appointed as vice president for university advancement at Cal State LA in 2014, having served as associate vice president for development at the University of the Pacific. She inherited a small advancement operation, with multiple vacant positions and few systems in place to support fundraising. The university was only raising about $5 million annually, compared with over $500 million at the nearby University of California Los Angeles (UCLA) (Gardner, 2018).

Cal State LA's advancement program was not unusual among regional state universities at that time. With the exception of flagship campuses, fundraising was still not a high priority for many public institutions across the country, including in California. Indeed, the state had discouraged its public universities from raising private money as recently as the 1990s.

Cal State LA enrolls many first-generation students, who generally do not come from wealthy backgrounds. For that reason, many people had viewed the potential for parent and alumni support to be limited, discouraging previous university administrations from making significant investments in fundraising staff or programs. The economic downturn in 2008 had made it even more difficult to secure resources for fundraising budgets (Gardner, 2018).

When Dial arrived at Cal State LA, a new president was in his first year and he was eager to move into what would be Cal State LA's first campaign. But there was much to be done in preparation. Dial quickly expanded the fundraising staff to include an associate vice president, five new directors of development, and additional staff in annual giving and prospect research. The structure is a hybrid, with gift officers reporting formally to the central office but with some having strong dotted lines to deans. The vice president for university advancement has responsibility for development and alumni relations and shares responsibility for communication and public affairs with the executive vice president of the university (Dial, 2021).

The Cal State LA Foundation was established in 1985 and is governed by a board of trustees that includes the university's president, vice president for advancement, and financial vice president, among other members (Cal State

LA, 2021d). The foundation receives and manages gifts, including endowment funds, but does not employ an independent staff.

ENGAGEMENT, SERVICE, AND THE PUBLIC GOOD

William A. Covino arrived as Cal State LA's seventh president in the fall, 2013, coming from the position of provost and vice president for academic affairs at Fresno State (Cal State LA, 2021e). A first-generation college graduate himself and a former English professor, Covino was a nationally known advocate of civic learning, "a process through which young people develop the knowledge, skills, and commitments to interact effectively with fellow community members to address shared problems" (*Leveraging Equity and Access*, 2021).

Making his agenda clear from the outset, Covino emphasized the university's engagement in the real world. "In my view, the key to our success and the success of every public university is, in a word, engagement," he said. "We have come a long way from the 'ivory tower' detachment that characterized many American universities during the last century" (Covino, 2013). He moved quickly to enlarge Cal State LA's connections with the community, establishing a new Center for Engagement, Service, and the Public Good to consolidate and strengthen community service and service-learning opportunities. He also created a new bioscience incubator to promote economic development in the region and entered a partnership with Los Angeles Mayor Eric Garcetti to help train civic and community leaders for the city (Cal State LA, 2021e).

In 2015, Covino launched a strategic planning process to formalize the university's directions and priorities. Led by a strategic planning coordinating committee, the process included focus groups, surveys, and other interactions with more than 2,600 students, faculty, and staff. The resulting plan set a clear goal: "Cal State LA will be internationally recognized as the premier comprehensive public university in greater Los Angeles." The plan focused on the university's mission of transforming lives and fostering community across Greater Los Angeles, articulating four key strategies:

- Graduate civic-minded students equipped for and committed to engagement, service, and the public good.
- Nurture a welcoming and inclusive campus where students, faculty, and staff thrive and community is honored and cultivated.
- Create a positive, holistic student experience with a clear and timely path to a high-quality degree.

- Provide high-quality undergraduate and graduate programs and investment in faculty who are uniquely committed to educating a diverse student body. (Cal State LA, 2021f)

WE ARE LA: THE CAMPAIGN FOR CAL STATE LA

Covino was clear that the new strategic plan would mark the beginning of a new era for the university. Achieving its goals would require a new era in fundraising as well—Cal State LA's *first comprehensive campaign*. With a modest fundraising history, little information on its potential donor base, and an advancement team that was just coming into place, preparing for the campaign would need to be on a fast track. Janet Dial would need to continue building the plane while flying it.

CAMPAIGN PLANNING AND STRATEGIES

One challenge was to reframe the case for support. As mentioned previously, fundraising had been an after-thought for many public institutions in California. Many alumni and other donors still perceived state universities as public goods, assuming that government funding was sufficient to meet the university's needs (Gardner, 2018). There also was a national trend of donors rethinking their giving priorities, focusing on the potential impact of their gifts on social causes and their communities as well as institutions (Worth et al., 2020).

About 70 percent of Cal State LA's students receive Pell grants, federal awards given to students demonstrating exceptional financial need. A university education is critical to their economic and social mobility and Cal State could point to many examples of students whose lives and careers had been shaped by their educational experience. Dial found that talking with donors about the success stories of such graduates elicited a more positive response than emphasizing the university's own institutional needs (Gardner, 2018).

She explains the reaction when she provided stories of the university's impact on graduates: "I can't tell you how many people have sat back in their chairs and said, 'That's me, That's me'" (Gardner, 2018). The social and economic mobility of the university's graduates would become the heart of the fundraising case, and stories of student and alumni success also would be become the centerpiece of its overall communications and branding.

Evaluating the Potential

As mentioned previously, Cal State LA lacked a significant fundraising history. Soon after her arrival, Dial had taken small steps to begin building a culture of philanthropy. She created a program for graduates to make a gift equivalent to their class year, for example, $20.18 from a member of the class of 2018. To expand annual giving, she initiated a call center staffed by students, who emphasized their personal accounts of the university's influence on their lives in their calls to potential donors (Gardner, 2018). But it would take years for such efforts to change the culture, and a campaign was just around the corner. A successful campaign would require securing major and principal gifts. Given the university's modest fundraising history, it was not known if there were potential donors in its constituency who could give at those levels.

The consulting firm Marts & Lundy was retained to conduct an analysis of the university's advancement database of 180,000 records to estimate the potential and identify prospective donors. The study concluded that the university's constituency might have the philanthropic *capacity* to give $75–100 million in a campaign. But there was little information on which to judge the other key variable—their *inclination* to give to Cal State LA.

In view of such uncertainty, the decision was made to set the campaign goal at the lower end of the consultant's suggested range—$75 million. That goal also would be symbolic, since the campaign was planned to end with the university's 75th anniversary celebration in 2022 (Dial, 2021).

Enlisting Volunteer Leadership

Two prominent alumni were enlisted as campaign co-chairs. Capri Maddox, Executive Director of the Los Angeles Department of Civil and Human Rights, had received both her bachelor's degree and a master's of public administration degree from Cal State LA. Given her position and responsibilities with the city government, she was particularly able to speak to the university's impact on the Los Angeles community. Richard D. Cordova had received his Cal State LA degree in business administration. As President and CEO of Children's Hospital Los Angeles, he was identified as one of the most influential individuals in his field, with strong relationships in the business community that could help open doors to potential campaign donors (Cal State LA, n.d.).

CAMPAIGN PRIORITIES

Campaign priorities were identified under four strategic pillars, closely aligned with priorities articulated in the university's strategic plan. As summarized in Table 5.1, the goals emphasized the diversity of the student body, inclusivity of the campus culture, student success, and community impact.

MOVING TO THE PUBLIC PHASE

The campaign was announced in 2018 at a major event at the university's Luckman Fine Arts Complex, featuring a video presentation, entertainment, and remarks from university officials and alumni. The campaign co-chairs and other alumni spoke to the role the university had played in advancing their lives and careers.

President Covino highlighted the historic moment—Cal State LA's first campaign—and emphasized its principal themes: "It's not a coincidence that the number one university for upward mobility is located in the heart of Los Angeles, a place that symbolizes change more than any other. . . . With the campaign that we launch tonight, we recognize Cal State LA's starring role on the stage that is Los Angeles" (Stewart, 2019).

The goal of $75 million was publicly announced at the kickoff event, with a nucleus fund of $40 million having been committed during the quiet phase (Beck, 2018).

Table 5.1. California State University, Los Angeles (Cal State LA). We Are LA: The Campaign for Cal State LA Campaign Priorities

Strategic Pillar	Goal
Academic Distinction	Provide high-quality undergraduate and graduate programs and investment in faculty who are uniquely committed to educating a diverse student body
Engagement, Service, and the Public Good	Graduate civic-minded students equipped for and committed to engagement, service, and the public good
Student Success	Create a positive, holistic student experience with a clear and timely path to a high-quality degree
Welcoming and Inclusive Campus	Nurture a welcoming and inclusive campus where students, faculty, and staff thrive and community is honored and cultivated

Source: Cal State LA. 2019a. We Are LA: The Campaign for Cal State LA. Website. https://campaign.calstatela.edu/ (accessed May 6, 2021).

PRINCIPAL GIFTS

Campaigns rely on major and principal gifts, which generally require well-established relationships with donors. Prospective donors at those levels usually meet three criteria: linkage with the institution, the financial capacity to make large gifts, and demonstrated interest in the institution's programs (Rosso, 1997). And the standard fundraising process includes cultivating the institution's relationship with prospective donors before proceeding to solicit a large gift, usually over a period of time. As discussed previously, Cal State LA did not have a long history of such engagement with donors. The Marts & Lundy analysis had identified the capacity for significant gifts among the university's constituency, but the depth of prospective donors' commitment to the university remained an unknown and a reason for caution in planning the campaign.

But three principal gifts instilled confidence and advanced the campaign beyond expectations. Two were from donors who had linkage with the university and who had made previous gifts. The third—and largest—commitment to the campaign was from a donor who was an established philanthropist, but not previously well-known to Cal State LA.

Dr. Rongxiang Xu was a scientist, surgeon, inventor, and humanitarian who grew up poor in China, completed medical school there, and eventually relocated to the Los Angeles area. Xu was best known for his development of a burn therapy that could restore patients' skin with less pain, illness, and death, a treatment that is now utilized by more than 200,000 doctors around the world (Gabrielle, 2019).

Dr. Xu had not had a relationship with Cal State LA when he passed away in 2015. But in 2016, the National Rongxiang Xu Foundation, managed by Dr. Xu's family, committed a $10 million gift, the largest in the university's history, to honor his memory and achievements (California State University Board of Trustees, 2016). The gift would be recognized through naming of the Rongxiang Xu College of Health and Human Services, the first named college at Cal State LA. The gift also would provide support for the Rongxiang Xu Bioscience Innovation Center, which would include an incubator enabling students and faculty to collaborate with biotech start-ups (Gabrielle, 2019).

The mission of Cal State LA resonated with Dr. Xu's life story. His son, Kevin Xu, a business leader and entrepreneur, explained that his father had grown up poor in China and was able to succeed because of help he received from others. "He didn't have a lot of resources and opportunities to become a success. . . . Eventually the people who believed in him provided him the opportunity and the platform [to succeed]" (Gabrielle, 2019).

Unlike Dr. Xu, Patricia Chin had a long history with Cal State LA. She was a Cal State LA alumna and faculty member, who had retired as director of the school of nursing. She and her husband William Chin, a physician, had been donors to the university since the 1970s. When Janet Dial met the Chins for lunch in 2015, William Chin explained that they had reached "the giveback phase" of their lives (Gardner, 2018).

Discussions with the Chins continued for the next couple of years and, in 2017, they announced a $7 million gift—the second largest in the university's history. Their gift would endow the Chin Family Institute for Nursing and create a state-of-the-art nursing simulation lab. In recognition of her career and philanthropy, the university named the Patricia A. Chin School of Nursing (Cal State LA, 2016).

Patricia Chin explained the gift in terms of her own career in nursing and the importance of hands-on training. The gift would support renovations and a director for the nursing simulation laboratory. And the Chin Family Institute for Nursing would focus on continuing education for nurses in the community, facilitate leadership in the nursing profession, and address regional and national health care policy (Beck, 2019).

Ronald H. Silverman had received a master's degree in art at Cal State LA in 1955 and went on to teach at the university for three decades, including service as chair of the Department of Art. Silverman had given previously to establish a scholarship fund for art students and for other purposes. In 2019, his son Jeffrey Silverman and daughter-in-law Amelia Perez-Silverman announced a planned gift of more than $1 million. Their gift would support students and a lecture series and would be recognized by naming of the Ronald H. Silverman Fine Arts Gallery, within the university's College of Arts and Letters (Cal State, 2019b).

Jeffrey Silverman had earned a bachelor's degree in biochemistry from Cal State LA and pursued a career in biopharmaceuticals. Amelia Perez-Silverman also was a Cal State LA graduate, with a bachelor's degree in environmental and health sciences, and had pursued a long career in education. Speaking at the event announcing their gift honoring his father, Jeffrey Silverman explained, "Even though we have science-based backgrounds, Amelia and I wanted to take this opportunity to support a critical but often overlooked part of a liberal arts education, and what better way than to support a gallery focused on exhibiting the work of both our students and community artists" (Cal State, 2019b).

CHALLENGES AND EARLY SUCCESS

By 2021, what had begun as somewhat of a gamble—a first campaign for a university with little fundraising history and a relatively undefined base of prospective donors—had achieved success ahead of schedule. Cal State LA reported that $83 million had been committed toward the campaign's $75 million goal.

It would not be uncommon for a university in that position to increase the campaign goal, or possibly even end the campaign early. But Cal State LA decided to keep the original goal and continue the campaign to its planned end date in 2022. As Janet Dial (2021) explains, the uncertainties of the economy and the Covid-19 pandemic argued against raising the goal. And concluding the campaign before the 75th anniversary in 2022 might forfeit an opportunity to celebrate both the campaign and the anniversary on that occasion.

Although the goal already had been exceeded, Dial was confident that donors would still be motivated to give during the campaign's final year, wishing to be part of Cal State LA's first campaign. Indeed, she attributed the campaign's success in part to the decision to promote it as a historic first and to blend campaign themes with the university's overall branding. The phrase "We Are LA" has been embraced by alumni and helped ignite overall institutional pride, while also becoming synonymous with the campaign (Dial, 2021).

Staffing Challenges

Despite the campaign's early success, there had been challenges along the way. One was difficulty in retaining development professional staff throughout the campaign. Gift officers at Cal State LA are compensated as state employees, in the context of a regional employment market that offers many opportunities, including positions at nearby private institutions with fewer constraints on compensation. The turnover of staff during the campaign required frequent adjustments to maintain continuity in donor relationships (Dial, 2021).

Adjusting to Covid-19

Like all institutions, Cal State LA was impacted by the Covid-19 pandemic in 2020 and 2021. The university switched to a virtual format for larger events and found some donors receptive to virtual visits. But the pandemic was a particular challenge for a university without long-established donor relationships. One strategy for donor cultivation that the university had been pursuing prior to the pandemic included a series of small, in-person events, for example, dinners at the president's home. Once Covid-19 hit, these events had to be suspended. Together with the problem of staff turnover, this complicated the important task of engaging new prospective donors for the campaign (Dial, 2021).

LESSONS LEARNED AND LOOKING TO THE FUTURE

By mid-2021, Cal State LA had succeeded in its first comprehensive campaign, with more than a year to go to the planned end date. Janet Dial was mindful that the consultant's original assessment had pointed to a range between $75 million and $100 million. With the campaign exceeding $83 million a year ahead of its planned conclusion, she was optimistic that the total would continue to increase, but was reluctant to hope that the higher number would be achieved. The challenges of building and sustaining the university's advancement program continued, as did aftershocks from the Covid-19 pandemic.

The campaign had brought increased visibility to philanthropy, attracted new donors, and helped establish a culture of philanthropy that would be important in future efforts. The linking of the campaign to the university's mission—community impact and social mobility—also had proven to be resonant with the national dialogue since the campaign's launch in 2014. The priorities of many donors had shifted to emphasize community impact and social justice, as evidenced in some nationally publicized mega gifts to other institutions. Cal State LA had positioned itself as an important force toward those purposes in the heart of the nation's second largest city.

What would come after the successful conclusion of We Are LA: The Campaign for Cal State LA? As the campaign entered its final year, Dial was focused on continuing the momentum that had been gained. That would include further expanding the development staff and continuing to expand annual and planned giving programs, which would be important in the post-campaign period.

Would there be a next campaign for Cal State LA? Without committing to the timing, Dial was certain there would be and pointed to the larger benefits of the campaign. The campaign had accomplished more than raising significant gifts; it had enhanced the university's visibility and brand and contributed to a stronger sense of community within the institution and its alumni. As Dial (2021) observes, "A campaign just gives a university an excuse to be louder and prouder."

REFERENCES

Beck, Jillian. 2018. "Cal State LA Launches First Comprehensive Fundraising Campaign." Press release, April 17. https://www.calstatela.edu/univ/ppa/publicat/cal-state-la-launches-first-comprehensive-fundraising-campaign (accessed May 6, 2021).

Beck, Jillian. 2019. "Shaping the Future of Nursing." *California State University, Los Angeles Magazine*, n.d. https://www.calstatelamagazine.com/features/patricia-chin-school-of-nursing (accessed May 18, 2021).

Cal State LA. n.d. "Health Care Administrator Richard Cordova '72 Offers a View from the Top." https://www.calstatela.edu/univ/ppa/publicat/today/issueSpecific/fall2009AlumniSpotlight.php (accessed June 8, 2021).

Cal State LA. 2016. "Cal State LA Receives $7 Million Gift to Name School of Nursing." Press release, December 2016. https://www.calstatela.edu/univ/ppa/publicat/cal-state-la-receives-7-million-gift-name-school-nursing (accessed May 18, 2021).

Cal State LA. 2018. "Cal State LA Selected as Anchor Institution for Nationwide CUMU Initiative." Press release, April 10. https://www.calstatela.edu/univ/ppa/publicat/cal-state-la-selected-anchor-institution-nationwide-cumu-initiative (accessed May 5, 2021).

Cal State LA. 2019a. *We Are LA: The Campaign for Cal State LA*. (Website) https://campaign.calstatela.edu/ (accessed May 6, 2021).

Cal State LA. 2019b. "Cal State LA Celebrates Naming of Ronald H. Silverman Fine Arts Gallery." Press release, May 9. https://www.calstatela.edu/univ/ppa/publicat/cal-state-la-celebrates-naming-ronald-h-silverman-fine-arts-gallery (accessed June 8, 2021).

Cal State LA. 2020. "Cal State LA Continues Impressive Rise in U.S. News & World Report Rankings." Press release, September 14. https://www.calstatela.edu/univ/ppa/publicat/cal-state-la-continues-impressive-rise-us-news-world-report-rankings (accessed May 17, 2021).

Cal State LA. 2021a. *Cal State LA History*. (Website) https://www.calstatela.edu/specialcollections/cal-state-la-history (accessed May 5, 2021).

Cal State LA. 2021b. *Academics*. (Website) https://www.calstatela.edu/academics (accessed May 5, 2021).

Cal State LA. 2021c. *CSULA Strengths in Diversity*. (Website) https://www.calstatela.edu/diversity/index-2007.htm (accessed May 5, 2021).

Cal State LA. 2021d. *Cal State LA Foundation*. (Website) https://www.calstatela.edu/advancement/foundation/committees-board (accessed May 6, 2021).

Cal State LA. 2021e. *President's Biography*. https://www.calstatela.edu/president/william-a-covino#:~:text=William%20A.,President%20Covino%20holds%20a%20Ph (accessed May 5, 2021).

Cal State LA. 2021f. *Cal State LA's Strategic Plan*. https://www.calstatela.edu/strategicplan (accessed May 6, 2021).

California State University Board of Trustees. 2016. *Committee on Institutional Advancement, Agenda*, May 24. https://www2.calstate.edu/csu-system/

board-of-trustees/past-meetings/2016/Documents/may-23-2016-institutional-advancement.pdf (accessed May 17, 2021).

Covino, William A. 2013. Remarks at University Convocation, September 23. https://www.calstatela.edu/sites/default/files/univ/ppa/covino-convocation2013.pdf (accessed June 1, 2021).

Dial, Janet Schellhase. 2021. Interview with author, June 7, 2021.

Gabrielle, Gwendolyn. 2019. "A Legacy Continues." *California State University Los Angeles Magazine*, n.d. https://www.calstatelamagazine.com/features/rongxiang-xu-la-biospace (accessed May 17, 2021).

Gardner, Lee. 2018. "In the Drive for Donors, Regional Public Colleges Have a Lot of Catching Up to Do." *Chronicle of Higher Education*, September 21 (www.chronicle.com).

Leveraging Equity and Access in Democratic Education (LEADE). 2021. https://centerx.gseis.ucla.edu/leade/civic-learning/ (accessed May 18, 2021).

Rosso, Henry A. 1997. *Achieving Excellence in Fund Raising*. Hoboken, NJ: Jossey-Bass.

Stewart, Jocelyn Y. 2019. "We Are LA." *California State University Los Angeles Magazine*, fall. https://www.calstatelamagazine.com/features/we-are-la-campaign (accessed May 6, 2021).

Worth, Michael J., Sheela Pandey, Sanjay K. Pandey, Suhail Qadummi. 2020. "Understanding Motivations of Mega-Gift Donors to Higher Education: A Qualitative Study." *Public Administration Review*, March/April, 80 (2), 281–293.

Chapter 6

Youngstown State University

WE SEE TOMORROW: THE CAMPAIGN FOR YOUNGSTOWN STATE UNIVERSITY

With a 145-acre campus located near the downtown of its namesake city in Ohio, Youngstown State University traces its founding to 1908, when the local YMCA started offering evening classes in commercial law in its own downtown building. That educational program expanded and became formalized, becoming Youngstown College in 1931 and gaining independence from the YMCA in 1944. By 1955, it became Youngstown University, remaining a private university until 1967, when it became publicly supported and changed its name to Youngstown State University (YSU). Today, YSU is governed by a board of trustees, appointed by the Governor of Ohio (History of YSU, n.d.).

Listed among Master's Colleges & Universities: Larger Programs in the Carnegie Classification, YSU offers more than 115 undergraduate programs and more than 40 graduate programs within seven academic units, including an Honors College, and also provides a variety of online programs. Historically a commuter campus serving primarily students from the Youngstown area, YSU maintains a substantial student aid program and prides itself on offering opportunities to students with limited financial resources (Youngstown State University, 2020a).

Athletics hold an important place in the life of YSU, which is known for the accomplishments of its nine men's and twelve women's varsity athletic teams. Since 1991, its football team, the Penguins, has won four national football championships (Youngstown State University, 2020a).

ADVANCEMENT AT YSU

The private Youngstown University had an endowment when it began considering state affiliation in 1966. Then university president Howard Jones sought to preserve the endowment in the university's transition to public control and established an independent 501(c) 3 organization to manage its assets, which primarily supported scholarships. He created the Youngstown Educational Foundation, which was renamed as the Youngstown State University Foundation in 1983, remaining a private entity governed by an independent board of trustees. By 2020, the foundation held over $275 million, making it the largest public university foundation in Northeast Ohio (Youngstown State University Foundation, 2020a).

Jones was the first president of the foundation and was followed by two long-serving successors. Paul J. McFadden became the fourth president of the foundation in 2012. McFadden had a long history with YSU, as an alumnus and former placekicker for the YSU Penguins football team, who went on to a career in the National Football League. He returned to YSU following his NFL career and served as the development officer for athletics. He later was appointed as the university's chief development officer, the position he held when he was named to lead the foundation (Youngstown State University, 2011).

Prior to 2014, YSU development operated as a unit within the university administration, with the foundation focused on management of endowment funds. Shortly after McFadden's move from the university staff to the foundation presidency, the university and the foundation agreed that the foundation would provide all development operations on behalf of the university, making the YSU Foundation "the designated philanthropic entity of Youngstown State University" (Youngstown State University Foundation, 2020a).

Gift officers are employees of the foundation, with some being assigned to serve particular schools and units. The Division of University Relations remains a part of the university structure, with responsibility for marketing, communications, alumni engagement, events, and a public radio station (Youngstown State University, 2020b). Public communication regarding campaigns and gifts is handled by a coordinator on the foundation's staff.

HISTORY OF CAMPAIGNS

YSU completed a comprehensive Centennial Campaign in 2010, directed by Paul McFadden during his tenure as chief development officer, which raised $47 million against its original $43 million goal (McFadden, 2021a). In addition to new endowed funds for scholarships and professorships, the campaign supported construction of a new building for the Williamson College of Business Administration and creation of the Watson and Tressel Training Site, a new athletic practice facility (Youngstown State University, 2010).

The new athletic facility was supported in part by a major gift from Ellen and James ("Jim") Tressel. Jim Tressel had served as YSU's head football coach for 15 years, leading the team to four national championships, and concurrently served as YSU's athletic director for six years during that period. In 2001, he left YSU to become head coach at the Ohio State University, where his teams won seven Big Ten championships and a national championship in 2002. He later went on to serve as Executive Vice President for Student Success at the University of Akron (Youngstown State University, 2020c).

When the Centennial Campaign concluded in 2010, both Jim Tressel and Paul McFadden were destined to play key roles in YSU's next chapter.

ENVISIONING YSU'S FUTURE

Youngstown and the surrounding Mahoning Valley have seen substantial economic and population decline over recent decades, accompanying the collapse of the U.S. steel industry that began in the 1970s. By the 2000s, efforts to rebuild were focused on the potential of higher education institutions to provide re-training and attract new industry to the region.

In 2007–2008, the Chancellor of the University System of Ohio released a system-wide strategic plan, which defined broad directions for Youngstown State University in relation to its community and region. YSU was identified as a critical resource in supporting the growth of new companies and industries, through increased research and economic impact (Youngstown State University, n.d.).

Responding to the system's mandate, in 2010, then YSU president Cynthia Anderson implemented a strategic planning process to determine the university's directions for 2011–2020. The resulting plan reaffirmed the university's mission and values and stated goals for that period of years (Youngstown State University, n.d.).

Anderson retired as president in 2013. Under an acting president the following year, the university suffered considerable turnover in administrative positions, experienced significant enrollment declines, and faced financial pressures that required budget cuts and layoffs (Tressel Inherits, 2014).

In 2014, the board of trustees announced that it was bringing Jim Tressel back to YSU as its ninth president. His appointment was not without some controversy. Some raised concerns from his coaching days and others noted that he had not risen through an academic career like most university presidents. But many saw Tressel as the right choice for YSU at that point in its history, pointing to his familiarity with the institution and the region and his successful tenure in the administration at the University of Akron. Some also predicted that his statewide renown might help YSU in fundraising and student recruitment by raising its visibility across the state and nationally (Botelho, Castillo, and Moorehead, 2014).

The new president soon articulated his own vision for YSU, described in a plan called "NextYSU." Noting YSU's declining enrollment and historic reliance on students from its local area, Tressel emphasized the need to increase recruitment and retention, strengthen academic quality, and extend the university's geographic reach. That would require the development of additional student housing, a stronger connection between the campus and downtown Youngstown, and improvements to the campus infrastructure and appearance, which reflected the budget cuts of recent years. Explaining his emphasis on improving the campus as essential to student recruitment, Tressel drew on his background in athletics, saying, "If [YSU] is going to be a player, it has to look like a player" (Jim Tressel Says Youngstown State, 2016).

Tressel's plan also included enhancing YSU's role in regional economic development, including new partnerships with local industry to foster entrepreneurship and growth (Youngstown State University, 2016).

WE SEE TOMORROW

Given declining state support and enrollment pressures, it was clear that increased philanthropy would be essential to achieving Tressel's goals. Planning for a new campaign began in 2014, shortly after his arrival.

CAMPAIGN PLANNING AND STRATEGIES

A consultant was retained to undertake a campaign planning study, including an analysis of the foundation's fundraising history and interviews with key donors and trustees. The study report recommended a working goal of $75–100 million for the quiet phase of the new campaign, with the decision on a public goal to be reached in two years. Many viewed the top of that range as ambitious, given YSU's history and economic conditions. It would be more than double the total attained in the previous campaign, much of which had been completed before the Great Recession. That economic downturn in 2009–2010 had significantly impacted the region, with lasting effects. But Tressel and the YSU Foundation board were determined to stretch and entered the quiet phase with the $100 million target in mind.

Historically, most students attending YSU had come from Northeast Ohio and nearby communities in Western Pennsylvania. Although a four-year institution that offered some graduate programs—and with a nationally known athletic program—YSU had functioned much like a community college for the Mahoning Valley. About half of the graduates remained in the region after graduation, but others scattered to other parts of the country.

The university had few relationships with alumni outside of the region and relatively little information about their interests and philanthropic capabilities. Most gifts to the foundation in previous years had come from local businesses and families, and the board of the foundation comprised primarily individuals living in Northeast Ohio. Campaign planners knew that expanding YSU's donor base and gaining more geographic reach would be essential.

The foundation completed an electronic wealth screening to identify new prospects among YSU alumni across the country who had the capacity for major and principal gifts and developed plans to engage with those individuals. The results of the screening were promising and, as discussed further later, the response of this constituency proved to be one of the positive surprises in the campaign (McFadden, 2021a).

CAMPAIGN LEADERSHIP AND MANAGEMENT

A single campaign committee was established, including members of the foundation board and other individuals who were major donors and were visible leaders in their communities. Alumna Jocelyne Kollay Linsalata, who chaired the YSU Foundation board, accepted the position of campaign chair as well. But most solicitations would be undertaken by Tressel, McFadden, and foundation gift officers, with some participation by deans and unit heads.

McFadden (2021a) emphasized the importance of putting "more boots on the ground" and expanded the foundation's staff to include new gift officers who would be capable of soliciting major and principal gifts to the campaign. The foundation's capabilities for prospect research, records, and reporting also were enhanced.

ENTERING THE PUBLIC PHASE

At a kickoff dinner in the fall of 2017, YSU publicly announced the "We See Tomorrow" campaign, the largest fundraising effort in its history, with a goal of $100 million to be raised by 2021. Linsalata announced that $51.7 million already had been committed during the quiet phase (Youngstown State University, 2017).

Among the lead gifts announced at the kickoff were a $2.5 million commitment from Morris and Phyllis Friedman, endowing a chair in engineering, and $2.5 million from the Fok family, in memory of Thomas Fok, a former YSU professor and trustee of the university and foundation (LaRue, 2017). And Jim and Ellen Tressel committed their own gift of $1 million, to establish the Tressel Student Work Opportunity Endowment Fund (Youngstown State University, 2015).

CAMPAIGN PRIORITIES

As summarized in Table 6.1, the comprehensive campaign objectives included annual giving, endowment, and specific projects, which closely tracked the NextYSU plan. Annual giving would comprise $20 million of the goal, followed by $20 million for student assistance, including both scholarships and work opportunities.

The emphasis on providing student work opportunities reflected Tressel's view, represented by his own campaign gift, that such opportunities were beneficial to students in multiple ways. "Research shows that students with part-time campus jobs are more successful in the classroom and have better chances of graduating on time," he explained, "not to mention the benefits of earning extra money for the variety of expenses that college presents" (Youngstown State University, 2015).

Consistent with Tressel's emphasis on improving the attractiveness of the campus, $10 million would be raised for campus beautification projects. Another $15 million would be raised for endowed professorships (Youngstown State University Foundation, 2020b). Programmatic priorities included the Mahoning Valley Innovation and Commercialization Center, including facilities and endowment, and a proposed Student Success Center that would bring together various student services in a common location.

The campaign also included $4 million for the Rich Center for Autism, a component of YSU's Beeghly College of Education (Youngstown State

Table 6.1. Youngstown State University. We See Tomorrow: Original Campaign Objectives (2017)

Objective	Goal
Student Success Center	$12 million
Mahoning Valley Innovation and Commercialization Center	$14 million
Scholarships and Student Work Opportunities	$20 million
Endowed Chairs and Professorships	$15 million
Campus Beautification	$10 million
Classrooms of the Future	$5 million
The Rich Center for Autism	$4 million
Annual Fund	$20 million
GOAL	$100 million

Source: Youngstown State University State Foundation. 2020b. *We See Tomorrow: The Campaign for Youngstown State University*. Website. https://weseetomorrow.ysufoundation.com/# (accessed February 8, 2021).

University Foundation, 2020b). The center had been established in 1995 by the Kosar, Rich (Ricchiuti), and Rubino families, in memory of Paula and Anthony Rich and their unborn child, victims of a plane crash in 1994, and provides education, training, research, and services to individuals affected by autism (Rich Center, 2017).

RAISING THE GOAL

In late 2020, the university announced that the $100 million campaign goal had been achieved—a year ahead of schedule. The total included 32 gifts of $1 million or more and $9.8 million committed by members of the YSU Foundation board. Rather than conclude the campaign early, the goal would be increased to $125 million, to be attained by the original end date in 2021 (Youngstown State University, 2020d).

REVISING PRIORITIES

While the $100 million goal had been reached overall, progress toward specific priorities had mixed results. Gifts for scholarships had exceeded expectations by a wide margin, with commitments triple the original $20 million goal. The number of endowed positions had increased from 3 to 17 and the annual fund had exceeded projections by more than 10 percent (McFadden, 2021a).

But the Student Success Center and the Mahoning Valley Innovation and Commercialization Center had proven less attractive to donors than had been anticipated. That required revisions in programmatic and funding strategies as well as a reordering of goals for the balance of the campaign, which are summarized in Box 6.1. The innovation center was re-designated as the Excellence Training Center and remained a priority for the campaign's final year. It also attracted significant government support, which was not included in campaign totals (McFadden, 2021a).

Soon after announcing the increase in the campaign goal, the YSU Foundation board announced a new initiative that also would become part of the campaign's final phase, securing endowment funds to create the President James P. Tressel Endowed Chair in Leadership. The chair would recognize "[Tressel's] ability to convene diverse groups and engage their support behind regional economic development projects [that has been] a catalytic force behind the Mahoning Valley's advancement over the past decade" ("YSU Foundation trustees establish endowed position," 2021).

> **BOX 6.1. YOUNGSTOWN STATE UNIVERSITY. WE SEE TOMORROW: PRIORITY INITIATIVES FOR ADDITIONAL $25 MILLION (2020)**
>
> - Student financial support, including scholarships and student work opportunities
> - Faculty enrichment, including endowed faculty chairs and endowed faculty professorships
> - Campus of Tomorrow, including Classrooms of the Future, the Excellence Training Center, campus beautification and the Success Center/Imagination Center "Think Box"
> - Distinctive collaborative opportunities, including medical professions, the arts and the Rich Center for Autism
>
> Source: Youngstown State University. 2020d. "YSU Increases 'We See Tomorrow' Goal to $125 Million." Press release, January 31. https://ysu.edu/news/ysu-increases-we-see-tomorrow-goal-125-million (accessed February 8, 2021).

CHALLENGES AND OPPORTUNITIES

As mentioned previously, one of the positive surprises was the response to the campaign by alumni outside of the Northeast Ohio region, many of whom had made no previous gifts and were relatively unknown to the university. Campaign chair Linsalata suggested that with the focus of the campaign on local impact, this group of donors may have responded as an expression of loyalty to their hometown (Linsalata, 2020).

"An Upside Down Campaign"

By early 2021, the campaign had achieved its original goal, but the lead gift of $5 million projected in the campaign plan had yet to be obtained. The plan had projected only 20 gifts above $1 million and 40 were received, making up the difference. Noting that this result is not the norm, Paul McFadden observed that "making up for the top gift with volume" is unlikely to be part of wise planning for most campaigns (McFadden, 2021a).

But as the campaign approached the official end date of the campaign in 2021, YSU announced a $5 million commitment from Dr. Chander M. Kohli and his spouse, Karen, providing equipment and technology enhancements to the newly constructed Excellence Training Center (ETC), to be named Kohli

Hall in recognition. Dr. Kohli, a prominent local neurosurgeon, had served as Chair of the Youngstown State University Board of Trustees and he and his spouse were members of the campaign cabinet.

The Kohlis' gift pushed the campaign total to more than $126 million, exceeding the *revised* goal of $125 by the *original* deadline. With the largest gift coming near the end rather than during the quiet phase, McFadden joked that YSU's campaign had been run "upside down" (McFadden, 2021b).

Facing Covid-19

Like all campaigns, We See Tomorrow was forced to allow for the Covid-19 pandemic beginning in 2020, which greatly reduced opportunities for in-person donor visits and events. Some donors were receptive to virtual visits, but others were not. Cultivation activities were seriously upended when the 2020 football season was curtailed, removing one of YSU's most important venues for events (McFadden, 2021a). In spring of 2020, the foundation launched a targeted "Penguin-to-Penguin" campaign to secure $50,000 to provide direct assistance to students adversely affected by the pandemic ("$50,000 campaign will help needy YSU students," 2020).

LESSONS LEARNED AND LOOKING TO THE FUTURE

One lesson of the We See Tomorrow campaign was the importance of presidential leadership. Jim Tressel played the primary role in defining the campaign priorities and developing its strategy. As the board of trustees had anticipated when appointing him, Tressel's visibility from his coaching days was a major draw, especially helpful in opening doors to newly identified prospects.

Cultivation activities included many small-group events, which attracted alumni and community leaders, many who were eager to spend time with the championship coach. These new relationships then provided opportunities for additional engagement and solicitations (McFadden, 2021a).

Reflecting on We See Tomorrow and looking forward to future campaigns, McFadden anticipates an increased emphasis on planned giving. Bequest expectancies were credited toward the campaign goal for donors age 65 and above, but cash receipts totaled nearly $83 million of the more than $100 million in commitments received by March 2021. McFadden characterized the campaign as "cash heavy" and expected that planned giving programs will be a greater focus in future YSU campaigns (McFadden, 2021a).

Perhaps the greatest lesson—and positive surprise—of the campaign was the extent to which YSU's emphasis on local and regional impact became a central motivation for both existing donors and the Youngstown "ex pats" who gave to advance their hometown. The lesson was not lost. By early 2021, McFadden was already planning to connect the YSU Foundation even more closely to community needs and was considering a new program for managing donor advised funds that would benefit YSU as well as other local organizations, possibly attracting interest from donors across the country (McFadden, 2021a).

Despite the significant expansion of its donor base and national exposure during the We See Tomorrow campaign, YSU would continue to be defined by its relationship with its community and its regional economic impact. That was the essence of its history and the heart of its case for support. As one foundation trustee expressed it, "YSU is the anchor tenant in downtown Youngstown and the region" and the best hope for economic recovery and growth (McFadden, 2021a).

NOTE: The author of this book advised YSU on campaign planning and conducted the campaign planning study as a consultant. No information obtained as a result of that relationship has been used in this case study unless otherwise available from public documents or provided independently by YSU for this purpose.

REFERENCES

Botelho, Greg, Mariano Castillo, and Jeremy Moorehead. 2014. "Jim Tressel—Ex-football Coach Rapped by NCAA—Offered School President Job." *CNN*, May 9. https://www.cnn.com/2014/05/09/us/ohio-jim-tressel-youngstown/index.html (accessed February 11, 2021).

"$50,000 Campaign Will Help Needy YSU Students." 2020. Press release, March 25. https://ysu.edu/news/50000-campaign-will-help-needy-ysu-students (accessed March 18, 2021).

History of YSU. n.d. William F. Maag, Jr. Library website. https://maag.guides.ysu.edu/c.php?g=532754&p=3819389#:~:text=Youngstown%20State%20University%20traces%20its,the%20Youngstown%20Institute%20of%20Technology (accessed February 6, 2021).

"Jim Tressel Says Youngstown State Needs to Look Like a Player." 2016. WKSU 89.7: Public Radio News for Northeast Ohio, April 22. https://www.wksu.org/community/2016-04-22/jim-tressel-says-youngstown-state-needs-to-look-like-a-player (accessed February 10, 2021).

LaRue, Dennis. 2017. "YSU Enters Public Phase of $100M Capital Campaign." *The Business Journal*, October 17. https://businessjournaldaily.com/ysu-enters-public-phase-of-100m-capital-campaign/ (accessed February 11, 2021).

Linsalata, Jocelyne Kollay. 2020. Interview. *The Business Journal*, January 30. https://www.youtube.com/watch?v=KrcQuoJWxDM (accessed March 5, 2021).

McFadden, Paul J. 2021a. Interview with author, March 18, 2021.

McFadden, Paul J. 2021b. Email to author, July 28, 2021.

Rich Center for Autism. 2017. About. http://richcenter.ysu.edu/about-us-2/ (accessed March 18, 2021).

"Tressel Inherits Financial Problems at Youngstown State." 2014. *The Columbus Dispatch*, June 7. https://www.dispatch.com/article/20140607/NEWS/306079866 (accessed February 12, 2021).

Youngstown State University. 2010. "It's All About Students," August 5. https://issuu.com/youngstownstate/docs/ysu_summer_2010_alumni_mag/23 (accessed February 8, 2021).

Youngstown State University. 2011. "McFadden Named President of YSU Foundation." Press release, November 17. http://newsroom.ysu.edu/paul-mcfadden-president-ysu-foundation/ (accessed February 6, 2021).

Youngstown State University. 2015. "Tressels Donate $1 Million to Establish Student Work Endowment Fund at YSU." Press release, November 16. http://newsroom.ysu.edu/tressels-donate-1-million-to-establish-student-work-endowment-fund-at-ysu/ (accessed March 18, 2021).

Youngstown State University. 2016. "NextYSU: Plan Outlines Campus Improvement," April 28. https://ysu.edu/news/nextysu-plan-outlines-campus-improvements (accessed February 8, 2021).

Youngstown State University. 2017. "YSU Announces $100 Million 'We See Tomorrow' Campaign; More Than Half of Goal Already Raised." Press release, October 25. https://ysu.edu/news/ysu-announces-100-million-we-see-tomorrow-campaign-more-half-goal-already-raised (accessed February 11, 2021).

Youngstown State University. 2020a. About. https://ysu.edu/about-ysu (accessed February 6, 2021).

Youngstown State University. 2020b. Division of University Relations website. https://ysu.edu/university-relations (accessed February 6, 2021).

Youngstown State University. 2020c. About James P. Tressel. https://ysu.edu/president/about (accessed February 8, 2021).

Youngstown State University. 2020d. "YSU Increases 'We See Tomorrow' Goal to $125 million." Press release, January 31. https://ysu.edu/news/ysu-increases-we-see-tomorrow-goal-125-million#:~:text=Jocelyne%20Kollay%20Linsalata%2C%20chair%20of,campaign%20goal%20of%20%24125%20million (accessed February 11, 2021).

Youngstown State University. n.d. *YSU 2020: The Strategic Plan of Youngstown State University 2011-2020*. https://ysu.edu/sites/default/files/YSU_strategic_booklet_final_2011_1.pdf (accessed February 8, 2021).

Youngstown State University Foundation. 2020a. About. https://ysufoundation.com/about-2/ (accessed February 6, 2021).

Youngstown State University State Foundation. 2020b. *We See Tomorrow: The Campaign for Youngstown State University.* (Website) https://weseetomorrow.ysufoundation.com/# (accessed February 8, 2021).

"YSU Foundation Trustees Establish Endowed Position in Honor of Jim Tressel." 2021. *Mahoning Matters*, January 28. https://www.mahoningmatters.com/local-news/ysu-foundation-trustees-establish-endowed-position-in-honor-of-jim-tressel-3303076 (accessed March 2, 2021).

PART III

Baccalaureate Colleges

The Carnegie Classification of Institutions of Higher Education identifies institutions as Baccalaureate Colleges if at least 50 percent of all the degrees they award are four-year bachelor's degrees. Some of these institutions may also award graduate degrees, but fewer than those classified as master's or doctoral universities. They are what many might view as a traditional definition of a "college," often with small enrollments and an intimate campus environment. Although some may think of these institutions simply as "liberal arts colleges," Carnegie divides them into two sub-categories: Arts & Sciences Focus and Diverse Fields. Most are private institutions.

Some colleges have national reputations and long histories of substantial philanthropy. Others are less visible and face the realities of smaller alumni bodies from which to enlist donors and few programs likely to attract corporate or foundation support. But the intimate nature of a small college and, in many cases, the unique niche that these institutions occupy, often instill a strong emotional commitment by those who are associated with them. Indeed, the top ten institutions in terms of alumni participation in 2020 included eight liberal arts colleges and two highly selective national universities (Moody, 2020).

The following two chapters in this section include case studies on comprehensive campaigns at baccalaureate colleges, both of which are private and classified as having a liberal arts focus. Both are distinctive and distinguished institutions.

ST. JOHN'S COLLEGE

St. John's College proudly identifies with the description offered by one journalist—"the most contrarian college in the country." With campuses in Maryland and New Mexico, its curriculum is focused on the study of Great Books. Like many small colleges, St. John's was facing financial and enrollment pressures that threatened its existence when, in 2018, it adopted a radically new financial model. Tuition would be significantly reduced and philanthropy would make up the difference. Rather than give financial aid in the form of tuition discounts, it would look to philanthropy as the source. In order to implement this plan, the college launched "Freeing Minds," a comprehensive campaign with a $300 million goal. The campaign kicked off with a $50 million challenge gift—the largest commitment in the college's history. By 2021, that challenge had been met, the campaign goal was in sight, and St. John's was anticipating record admissions and a balanced budget.

SPELMAN COLLEGE

Spelman College, in Atlanta, is the leading institution dedicated to the education of women of African descent and is ranked number one among Historically Black Colleges and Universities (HBCU). The college is named for the spouse of John D. Rockefeller, who was its early benefactor. In more recent years, Spelman has broadened its base of support and completed successful campaigns. In 2020, the college announced "Spelman Ascends," with a goal of $250 million to be achieved by 2024. On the occasion of the campaign's announcement, 96 percent of the goal already had been achieved. Among other principal gifts, the campaign had benefited from the widely publicized philanthropy of MacKenzie Scott, who gave $800 million to colleges serving "historically marginalized and underserved people" (Redden, 2021). Despite its early success, Spelman intended to continue the campaign to its original closing date in 2024, with an emphasis on strengthening annual and planned giving.

REFERENCES

Moody, Josh. 2020. "10 Colleges Where the Most Alumni Donate." *US News & World Report*, December 8. https://www.usnews.com/education/best-colleges/the-short-list-college/articles/universities-where-the-most-alumni-donate (accessed July 6, 2021).

Redden, Elizabeth. 2021. "A Fairy Godmother for Once-Overlooked Colleges." *Inside Higher Ed*, January 4. https://www.insidehighered.com/news/2021/01/04/mackenzie-scott-surprises-hbcus-tribal-colleges-and-community-colleges-multimillion#:~:text=A%20Fairy%20Godmother%20for%20Once,those%20from%20low%2Dincome%20backgrounds (accessed May 10, 2021).

Chapter 7

St. John's College

FREEING MINDS: A CAMPAIGN FOR ST. JOHN'S COLLEGE

St. John's College is the third oldest institution of higher education in the United States, tracing its history to the founding of The King William's School in Annapolis, Maryland, in 1696. Chartered as St. John's College in 1784, its founders included four signers of the Declaration of Independence. The original campus in Annapolis is in the center of a picturesque waterfront community near the U.S. Naval Academy. A second campus in Santa Fe, New Mexico, was opened in 1964, and is located amidst that city's vast artistic and cultural scene (St. John's College, 2021a).

Classified by Carnegie among Baccalaureate Colleges: Arts & Sciences Focus, St. John's offers undergraduate and master's degrees, as well as graduate certificates and a combined MA/JD program with the University of Maryland. The college is governed by a Board of Visitors and Governors. Although St. John's is a private institution, the board includes the governors of Maryland and New Mexico.

St. John's distinctive curriculum is focused on the reading of Great Books, which include "the foundational texts of Western civilization" (St. John's College, 2021a). With about 900 students across both campuses, classes are small and emphasize "collaborative inquiry" and discussions. Faculty members, who are known as "tutors," function as guides and model learners, rather than primarily content experts or lecturers. Their goal "is not to transmit information, but to pose questions that further students' ability to develop as thinkers in their own right" (St. John's College, 2021a).

St. John's has distinctive traditions and its own lingo. The curriculum is known simply as "The Program." Students and alumni are called "Johnnies" and all classrooms include the same wooden chairs, known as "Johnnie Chairs." Instead of receiving grades, students meet with their tutors in what is called a "Don Rag" to receive an oral review of their performance (St. John's College, 2021a).

In a 2018 article, *New York Times* opinion columnist Frank Bruni called St. John's "the most contrarian college in America," a characterization that the college embraced with pride. As Bruni explained, "[St. John's is] an increasingly exotic and important holdout against so many developments in higher education—the stress on vocational training, the treatment of students as fickle consumers, the elevation of individualism over a shared heritage—that have gone too far. It's a necessary tug back in the other direction."

ADVANCEMENT AT ST. JOHN'S

The administrative structure of St. John's is complex, with two campuses, two presidents and two vice presidents who hold fundraising responsibilities. The two campuses operated with independent administrations until 2016. Mark Roosevelt joined St. John's as president of the Santa Fe campus that year and was named college-wide president soon after. His expanded responsibilities encompassed college-wide administrative affairs, including advancement and financial management, as well as programs on the Santa Fe campus. Both campus presidents report to the Board of Visitors and Governors, as do the deans (St. John's College, 2021b).

Known for his commitment to social activism, Roosevelt is the great grandson of President Theodore Roosevelt. With undergraduate and law degrees from Harvard, he pursued a career in Massachusetts politics, serving as a member of the Massachusetts State Legislature and a gubernatorial candidate in 1994, then went on to a career in public education in Pittsburgh. In 2011, he was appointed president of Antioch College, a liberal arts institution in Ohio that had closed in 2008. Roosevelt presided over Antioch's reopening and revival before moving on to St. John's (St. John's College, 2021c).

Kelly Brown is St. John's vice president of advancement and campaign director, based on the Annapolis campus. Brown was appointed to her position in 2018, following positions at the University of Maryland and Johns Hopkins. She reports to college-wide president Roosevelt with regard to her responsibilities for principal and major gifts, planned giving, and the campaign. In addition to those college-wide responsibilities, she manages community relations in the Annapolis area and reports to the Annapolis president with regard to those programs.

Phelosha Collaros joined St. John's in 2016 as vice president for development and alumni relations, after serving as director of the foundation of the American Society of Radiologic Technologists. She is an alumna of St. John's and was the volunteer president of the college's alumni association prior to her appointment. Based on the New Mexico campus and also reporting to Roosevelt, Collaros is responsible for annual giving, alumni relations, advancement services, and board relations. Communications and marketing programs are managed by a vice president of communications and creative strategy, who is based in New Mexico and serves both campuses.

PREVIOUS CAMPAIGNS

St. John's has completed campaigns in the past, especially focused on endowment to support financial assistance to students. A $125 million campaign, "With a Clear and Single Purpose," was announced in 2006, with a nucleus fund of $71 million, and closed in 2008 having raised more than $133 million (Olson, 2006; St. John's College, 2008). The campaign was chaired by alumnus Ron Fielding, who made a $10 million lead gift (St. John's College, 2008).

In reflecting on that campaign, Fielding highlighted some challenges inherent in St. John's fundraising environment, many of which would continue to be relevant in future years. The St. John's alumni constituency is smaller than that of many liberal arts colleges. While the Annapolis campus is among the oldest institutions in the country, some alumni of the Santa Fe campus had graduated as recently as 1968. By the mid-2000s, many remained relatively young and few had the capacity to make major gifts.

As Fielding observed, those realities gave added importance to large lead gifts and made it essential to reach beyond alumni to friends of the college, which included participants in Executive Seminars in Annapolis and Summer Classics programs in Santa Fe (St. John's College, 2008).

Despite the challenges, "With a Clear and Single Purpose" had exceeded its original goal. But the need for philanthropy would become even more important as the college initiated a new financial model in 2018.

IMPLEMENTING A PHILANTHROPY-CENTERED MODEL

Tuition at American colleges, especially private institutions, has increased at three times the rate of inflation for decades. Rising tuition reflects in part rising costs, a problem especially acute for an institution like St. John's, which intentionally maintains a small enrollment, small classes, and a full-time faculty.

But, according to Mark Roosevelt, increased tuition in higher education also may reflect a marketing strategy that some institutions have employed. As he explains, "For too long, most private colleges have been driven by the idea that families believe high price equals high quality, and with this belief private colleges have embraced an escalating tuition model known as 'prestige pricing'" ("St. John's Commits," 2018).

Sometimes called the high tuition/high aid model, the prevailing system has long been a source of debate among higher education experts and economists (Turner, 2018). While many colleges advertise a high sticker price, some portion of the tuition is offset by financial aid for many or most students. That reduces the actual price they pay. However, as St. John's vice president for enrollment management argues, the result could be confusion and counter-productive. Not all prospective students might understand how this model works and some could be discouraged from even considering a college like St. John's with a high posted tuition rate (Valbrun, 2019).

By 2018, the old model was no longer working for St. John's. The college's cost-per-student had reached $60,000, while tuition was about $52,000, leaving a significant gap that resulted in operating deficits ("St. John's Commits," 2018). As Kelly Brown (2021) explains, the student body at St. John's was bifurcated into "full-pay and full-aid," resulting in net revenue inadequate to support the college's operations. Something had to change.

St. John's made a big decision. Beginning in the fall of 2019, tuition would be reduced to $35,000, without substantially increasing enrollment or reducing financial aid, and budgets would be balanced over a period of five years. Increased philanthropy would make up the difference. The plan was not without risk. Other colleges had tried reducing tuition but with varied success. Some had cut financial aid too much and lost enrollment. Others had overshot on maintaining financial aid and suffered a decline in total revenue (Valbrun, 2019). St. John's would need to thread the needle and avoid these negative outcomes.

By 2021, St. John's new model seemed to be working. Despite the impact of the Covid-19 pandemic, the college was anticipating record admissions and a balanced budget for the 2021–2022 academic year (Brown, 2021).

FREEING MINDS

What was unique—and audacious—about St. John's strategy was that it would move away from a tuition-driven revenue model to one driven by philanthropy. A new campaign would be critical to its success.

CAMPAIGN PLANNING AND STRATEGY

Preliminary planning began in 2015 and the new campaign moved into its quiet phase in 2016, when it received a major early boost from two principal gifts announced at the fall meeting of the Board of Visitors and Governors. Ron Fielding, who had chaired the previous campaign and was now the board chair, and Warren Spector, chair of the new campaign, each announced a gift of $25 million. The total of $50 million would support financial aid to students who could not otherwise afford St. John's; add to the college's endowment; provide ongoing support for academics and career services; and increase the school's annual fund (⊠St. John's Receives $50 Million," 2016).

Both Fielding and Spector had been involved with St. John's philanthropy for a long time. Spector, who was chairman of private investment firm Balbec Capital, had been a major donor to the college in the past. That included funding for Spector Hall, a residence hall named after his father, Philip Spector (Nott, 2016). Based on his experience as a major donor and chair of the previous campaign, Fielding understood the importance and potential impact of early lead gifts.

Fielding expressed hope that the two new gifts would provide leverage. As he had observed a decade earlier, there would be a need for support from college friends as well as increased participation by alumni. "This commitment is our rallying cry to fellow board members, alumni, and friends at the dawn of our capital campaign," he said. "It's a signal of confidence in the college's direction and a call to action. While $50 million is an important foundation for the future of St. John's College, it is only the beginning. We are calling on fellow supporters of 'the Program' to come forward, and we hope to inspire gifts both large and small" ("St. John's Receives $50 Million," 2016).

The consulting firm Creative Fundraising Advisors was retained to complete a feasibility study and an analysis of St. John's donor base and to advise on campaign planning. Despite the strong start, there was work to be done and uncertainty about what would be a realistic campaign goal.

BUILDING A CULTURE OF PHILANTHROPY

Although it had completed previous successful campaigns, St. John's did not have a well-established culture of philanthropy and lacked some of the fundraising infrastructure that would generally be necessary for a campaign, including strong programs for prospect research, planned giving, and donor stewardship. The financial pressures facing the college were causing budget reductions in many areas, and identifying the increased resources needed to support the campaign also presented a challenge (Brown, 2021). The capacity of the relatively small alumni base remained uncertain and donor reactions to the planned new financial model were not entirely predictable. The circumstances called for caution.

A working goal was established in the range of $250–300 million and there was continuing discussion and debate about how far to stretch. The debate continued until just a week before the planned announcement, when a significant new commitment was finalized and tipped the balance in the direction of optimism.

KICKOFF WITH A CHALLENGE

The public phase of "Freeing Minds" was launched in the fall of 2018 with a $300 million goal, to be achieved by 2023. The college did not hold a traditional kickoff event, but announced the campaign on the same day that Frank Bruni's (2018) front-page article in the *New York Times* was published. The article captured wide visibility and fostered pride within the St. John's community, adding excitement to the campaign announcement.

The campaign nucleus fund of $183 million included the largest single commitment in St. John's history, adding early momentum and building confidence in the $300 million goal. The Winiarski Family Foundation would match every gift to Freeing Minds—up to a total of $50 million—with an equivalent contribution to the college endowment ("St. John's College Receives $50 Million," 2018).

Warren and Barbara Winiarski had met while students at St. John's in Annapolis. Warren Winiarski owned the renowned Acadia Vineyards and was the founder of Stag's Leap Wine Cellars, based in California's Napa Valley. Barbara Winiarski had been among the first class of women admitted to St. John's. She had worked alongside her husband in building his business and also was renowned as a painter and writer. Both attributed their success to their college experience and described their gift as an effort to provide a similar opportunity to future generations. As Warren Winiarski explained, "My St. John's education enabled me to acquire the proficiency and skills I needed . . ." (St. John's College, 2021d).

CAMPAIGN PRIORITIES

As shown in Table 7.1, two-thirds of the $300 million campaign goal, $200 million, was intended to increase the St. John's endowment, doubling its value and providing an estimated $10 million in new annual income for scholarships and the operating budget. Another $50 million included annual giving over the campaign period, identified as part of the plan to reduce operating deficits and achieve "operating stability" under the new financial model. And $50 million would meet essential facilities needs at both the Annapolis and Santa Fe campuses (St. John's College, 2021d).

Demonstrating its contrarian nature that Frank Bruni (2018) had identified, St. John's campaign materials claimed, "The Freeing Minds campaign is as different from the campaigns of other schools as our Program is from their educational offerings. This is not an effort aimed at the big, the expensive, and the unnecessary. It is the fuel for continuing the Great Conversation" (St. John's College, 2021d).

COMPLETING THE CHALLENGE

By the spring of 2021, the campaign had achieved $245 million in total commitments, and had completed securing the gifts needed to complete the Winiarski Challenge. Priorities for the campaign's final three years were refined to include a greater emphasis on endowment and facilities improvements (Brown, 2021).

The Winiarski Challenge had significant impact, generating 17,000 new gifts, 20 percent of whom were new, and a record-breaking giving day in 2020 (Brown, 2021). One response to the challenge was a $10 million gift from the Jay Pritzker Foundation, which established the Pritzker Promise Bridge Program. That program includes a summer session focused on assisting Pell Grant recipients and underrepresented incoming students on both campuses to develop academic skills and study habits and build relationships with faculty and peers prior to beginning the fall opening seminar (Mira, 2020).

CHALLENGES AND OPPORTUNITIES

As mentioned previously, St. John's philanthropic culture, its small alumni body, and its complex administrative structure established the environment

Table 7.1. St. John's College. Freeing Minds: Campaign Priorities

Endowment	$200 million
Financial Stability (annual fund)	$50 million
Campus Improvements	$50 million
GOAL	$300 million

Source: St John's College. 2021d. Freeing Minds Website. https://freeingminds.sjc.edu/our-solution/ (accessed March 22, 2021).

for campaign planning. Some elements of fundraising infrastructure needed enhancement and budgetary pressures made it difficult to identify the resources needed to build the program. Arriving in 2016, while the campaign was already in its quiet phase, Kelly Brown had to build a plane while flying it—and to do so with limited resources.

Managing across Two Campuses

There were identified needs on both St. John's campuses. But the Annapolis campus had the advantage of an older and wealthier alumni body and also had access to other resources. The latter included the possibility of Maryland state support for facilities projects and annual revenue from the Hodson Trust. Established in 1920 by business leader Thomas S. Hodson, the trust distributes scholarship funds annually to four Maryland institutions: Johns Hopkins University, Hood College, Washington College, and St. John's (Hodson Trust, n.d.).

The Santa Fe campus, in existence for just decades, faced many needs, including updating of some of its original facilities. But Santa Fe alumni still were generally younger than those of the original campus in Annapolis, with less philanthropic capacity, and Santa Fe did not have the same access to public support or a guaranteed annual infusion of philanthropy. These different histories and circumstances complicated the task of matching donor capacity and interests with funding priorities across the two campuses.

Responding to Covid-19

The beginning of the Covid-19 pandemic in 2020 led St. John's to introduce new fundraising initiatives, including a Student Emergency Relief Fund that raised more than $77,000 to assist students facing hardships (St. John's College, 2020). The pandemic also required adapting operations to a suddenly changed environment. Staff meetings, events, and other activities went virtual and personal visits with donors became difficult to accomplish. But, as Brown (2021) notes, the situation actually offered some advantages for St. John's.

For one, suspension of campaign events and travel provided a window for re-focusing on building the fundraising infrastructure mid-campaign. That included strengthening programs for planned giving and foundation support and establishing metrics for development staff. And virtual meetings that included staff on two sides of the country actually helped build the team and improve communications—as Brown describes, the move to the virtual environment enabled "crossing boundaries" (Brown, 2021).

Looking ahead in 2021, Brown noted that donor contacts and events in the future will require more effort than in the past. While some events return to in-person, there will be a continuing need for a virtual component as well. Abandoning that approach following the pandemic would mean that individuals who became engaged virtually during that time would again become isolated. The point is especially important for St. John's. Many institutions have alumni living in relatively large numbers in concentrated locations, making large in-person events feasible. But St. John's has a smaller number of alumni scattered across the country. Ongoing virtual access would be essential for continuing to engage them (Brown, 2021).

LESSONS LEARNED AND LOOKING TO THE FUTURE

By mid-2021 Brown was optimistic that Freeing Minds was on track to reach its goal by 2023. Indeed, the philanthropic capacity and commitment of Johnnies revealed during the campaign had been a positive surprise. While still seeking the gifts needed to reach the $300 million campaign goal, St. John's also was planning for the post-campaign period. That would require increasing alumni engagement, building the annual giving program, and strengthening stewardship programs (Brown, 2021).

Brown was already thinking about the next campaign, sometime after 2023. But uncertainties abounded. The college announced in 2021 that Annapolis president Pano Kanelos would not be serving another term and that a search for his successor had been launched (St. John's College, 2021e). In addition to new leadership, St. John's would be facing a national environment still challenging to small, private colleges. Although she remained optimistic about St. John's future, Brown (2021) noted predictions that many such institutions could fail in the coming decade, perhaps affecting confidence and giving to those that survive.

Only one thing seemed certain—that St. John's would continue to be unique—and contrarian.

REFERENCES

Brown, Kelly. 2021. Interview with author, April 20, 2021.

Bruni, Frank. 2018. "The Most Contrarian College in America." *New York Times*, September 11. https://www.nytimes.com/2018/09/11/opinion/contrarian-college-stjohns.html (accessed March 23, 2021).

Hodson Trust. n.d. Website. http://www.hodsontrust.org/shipinfo.html (accessed April 20, 2021).

Mira, Abdullah. 2020. "St. John's College Launches Pritzker Challenge." Press release, October 28. https://www.sjc.edu/news/st-johns-college-launches-pritzker-promise-program (accessed April 20, 2021).

Nott, Robert. 2016. "Record $50M donated to St. John's College." *Santa Fe New Mexican*, November 7. https://www.santafenewmexican.com/news/local_news/record-50m-donated-to-st-john-s-college/article_5193a55e-9d73-5a15-b6ee-d693759ee649.html (accessed March 23, 2021).

Olson, Bradley. 2006. "College Starts Funding Drive." *Baltimore Sun*, April 26. https://www.baltimoresun.com/news/bs-xpm-2006-04-26-0604260185-story.html (accessed March 22, 2021).

St. John's College. 2008. *The Campaign for St. John's College: With a Clear and Single Purpose*. https://www.yumpu.com/en/document/view/26750969/as-the-college-prepares-to-successfully-close-its-st-johns-college (accessed April 20, 2021).

St. John's College. 2020. *Freeing Minds: Campaign Impact Report*. https://1vtuku1mvnfp1g4lfn2xgtpc-wpengine.netdna-ssl.com/wp-content/uploads/2020/06/SJC_Freeing_Minds_Campaign_Report_Spring_2020.pdf (accessed March 25, 2021).

St. John's College. 2021a. About. https://www.sjc.edu/about (accessed July 8, 2021).

St. John's College. 2021b. Leadership. https://www.sjc.edu/about/leadership (accessed July 8, 2021).

St. John's College. 2021c. Santa Fe President. https://www.sjc.edu/about/leadership/presidents/santa-fe-president (accessed March 31, 2021).

St. John's College. 2021d. Freeing Minds. https://freeingminds.sjc.edu/ (accessed July 8, 2021).

St. John's College. 2021e. Annapolis Presidential Search. https://www.sjc.edu/presidential-search (accessed July 29, 2021).

"St. John's College Commits to Affordability with New Financial Model." 2018. *Businesswire*, September 12. https://www.businesswire.com/news/home/20180912005349/en/St.-John%E2%80%99s-College-Commits-to-Affordability-with-New-Financial-Model (accessed March 23, 2021).

"St. John's College Receives $50 Million Toward New Tuition Model." 2018. *Philanthropy News Digest*, September 18. https://philanthropynewsdigest.org/news/st.-john-s-college-receives-50-million-toward-new-tuition-model (accessed March 24, 2021).

"St. John's Receives $50 Million in Gifts." 2016. *Philanthropy News Digest*, November 8. https://philanthropynewsdigest.org/news/st.-john-s-college-receives-50-million-in-gifts (accessed April 22, 2021).

Turner, Sarah. 2018. "The Evolution of the High Tuition, High Aid Debate." *Change: The Magazine of Higher Learning*, 50 (3–4), 142–148.

Valbrun, Marjorie. 2019. "A New Model for a New Reality." *Inside Higher Education*, October 28. https://www.insidehighered.com/news/2019/10/28/st-johns-college-tuition-cut-reaps-increased-applications-and-donations (accessed March 23, 2021).

Chapter 8

Spelman College

SPELMAN ASCENDS: A CAMPAIGN FOR SPELMAN COLLEGE

In 1818, Baptist missionaries Sophia B. Packard and Harriet E. Giles traveled from their homes in Massachusetts to Atlanta, Georgia, to start a new school for recently freed Black women. Rev. Frank Quarles, known as Father Quarles, offered space in the basement of his Friendship Baptist Church, where Packard and Giles established the Atlanta Baptist Female Seminary.

In its early decades, the school was funded primarily with small gifts from local women and churches. Then, one Sunday in 1882, Sophia Packard was speaking at a church service in Cleveland, hoping to raise additional funds. John D. Rockefeller was in the congregation. On the following day, Packard and Giles were invited to spend the afternoon at the Rockefellers' home. Rockefeller offered his financial support and continued to give to the school over the following years (Spelman College, 2020a).

In 1924, the seminary was renamed to recognize his support and to honor the family of his spouse, Laura Spelman Rockefeller. Her parents, Harvey Buel and Lucy Henry Spelman, had worked for the abolition of slavery and equal rights for Black people. They had provided shelter to runaway slaves in their home in Ohio and had been advocates for public school reform and women's rights. Rockefeller continued to be personally involved as a donor and board member at Spelman throughout his lifetime (Spelman College, 2020a).

Today, Spelman College is the leading institution in the education of women of African descent. It ranks at the top as a producer of Black women who complete Ph.Ds. in science, technology, engineering, and math (STEM) disciplines and in the top ten for social mobility and innovation. In 2021, *U.S. News and World Report* ranked Spelman number one in Historically Black Colleges and Universities (HBCU) for the fourteenth straight year (Spelman College, n.d.-a). The term "HBCU" was established in the Higher Education Act of 1965 and includes institutions founded before 1964 to serve Black students, who were generally prevented from attending other colleges and universities because of racial discrimination.

Spelman offers a range of academic majors and programs on its scenic campus just outside downtown Atlanta. It also is part of the Atlanta University Center Consortium, which includes Clark Atlanta University, Morehouse College, and Moorehouse School of Medicine. Spelman students have expanded study opportunities through that consortium as well as partnerships with various other colleges and universities (Spelman College, n.d.-a).

Some notable Spelman alumnae include Children's Defense Fund founder Marian Wright Edelman; Rosalind Brewer, chief executive officer of Walgreens Boots Alliance; political leader Stacey Abrams; former Acting Surgeon General and Spelman's first alumna president Audrey Forbes Manley; actress and producer Latanya Richardson Jackson; global bioinformatics geneticist Janina Jeff; and authors Pearl Cleage and Tayari Jones (Spelman College, n.d.-a).

Spelman has a rich history that has impacted the nation, including the activism of its students and alumnae in the movement to end segregation. In 1957, accompanied by history professor Howard Zinn, students from Spelman protested segregation of seating in the Georgia legislature, and Spelman students were there to celebrate when desegregation in that facility was finally ended in 1963 (Lefever, 2005). Women from Spelman also were among those arrested with Dr. Martin Luther King Jr. when protesting a segregated department store in Atlanta. King wrote to them from jail, "It is inspiring enough to see the fellows willingly accepting jail instead of bail, but when young ladies are willing to accept this type of self-suffering for the cause of freedom, it is both majestic and sublime" (Campbell, 2016).

ADVANCEMENT AT SPELMAN

Jessie L. Brooks was appointed as Spelman's vice president for institutional advancement in 2016. A native of New Mexico and an engineer by background, Brooks had over 20 years of experience in advancement in higher education. He most recently had served as senior director of development for the Scripps Institution of Oceanography at the University of California, San Diego, and previously had held advancement leadership positions at the Thunderbird School of Global Management, the University of Washington College of Engineering, and San Diego State University.

A few years after Brooks's arrival and upon retirement of Spelman's long-serving vice president for college relations, President Mary Schmidt Campbell initiated a reorganization. Programs previously managed by the office of college relations were redistributed to various divisions. Alumnae engagement programs and fundraising were consolidated in the office of institutional advancement, under Brooks's direction (Brooks, 2021).

PREVIOUS CAMPAIGNS

HBCUs historically have struggled to raise funds because of African Americans' lack of access to wealth and discrimination on the part of many individual and institutional donors. As Marybeth Gasman, a scholar who studies HBCUs, observed in 2010, "Theirs is a storied history of garnering funds from wealthy White philanthropists, the Black church, and as of late, their alumni who are not used to giving regularly because they have not been asked."

Despite these realities, Spelman has enjoyed some notable fundraising successes, moving beyond the historic support of the Rockefeller family foundations (Peeples, 2010). A campaign in the 1990s, during the presidency of Johnnetta B. Cole, Spelman's first Black female president, raised $138 million (Peeples, 2010). But the campaign had relied on a few significant gifts from foundations and philanthropists in the northeast and did not see broad participation by alumnae, reflecting the conditions that Gasman noted (McAllister-Grande, 2015).

Beverly Daniel Tatum became Spelman's president in 2002, having served as a philosophy professor and acting president at Mount Holyoke College. In 2004, following a study by the consulting firm Washburn and McGoldrick, she launched a comprehensive campaign focused on scholarship support, academic initiatives, and campus facilities. That campaign concluded in 2014, having secured $157.8 million—a new record for Spelman.

The total included a $17 million gift to create the Gordon-Zeto Center for International Education, in honor of two distinguished Spelman alumnae. But the campaign also had expanded alumnae participation. Of the 18,000 gifts received during the campaign, 12,000 came from Spelman alumnae (Spelman College, 2014).

IMAGINE, INVENT, ASCEND

Tatum retired in 2015, following conclusion of the campaign. Mary Schmidt Campbell was a professor and former dean at the Tisch School of the Arts at New York University. She was renowned in the New York arts community, having led the transformation of the Studio Museum in Harlem and later serving as vice chairwoman of the President's Committee on the Arts and Humanities under President Barack Obama. Campbell was already known to people at Spelman, having provided advice on a planned renovation of its art facilities. In 2015, the board of trustees selected her as Spelman's tenth president (Connley, 2015).

Campbell's vision for the college was unveiled in her inaugural address. Acknowledging the college's achievements and standing, she pointed to the need to enhance outcomes—increasing the graduation rate, teaching the language and tools of technology, and preparing students to work globally. "As good as Spelman has become," she spoke, "we have to do more, we have to be more" (Campbell, 2016).

Campbell's inaugural call to action was soon embodied in a new strategic plan with a bold goal: "Grounded in our compelling mission and value propositions, we will propel Spelman College into the top tier of liberal arts institutions" (Spelman College, 2018a). Titled "Imagine, Invent, Ascend," the plan covered the years 2017 to 2022 and encompassed various objectives organized under four priorities: Delivering the Spelman Promise, Elevating the Spelman Difference, Enhancing Operational Excellence, and Promoting Academic Innovation. These priorities also would become pillars for a new comprehensive campaign (Spelman College, 2018a).

SPELMAN ASCENDS

In March 2021—in a virtual event amidst the Covid-19 pandemic—Spelman announced the largest campaign in its history. Having begun in 2017, "Spelman Ascends" would continue to 2024, with a goal of $250 million.

CAMPAIGN PLANNING AND STRATEGY

Spelman had engaged a local consulting firm to conduct a feasibility study for the campaign. The feasibility study resulted in recommendation of a goal in the $200–250 million range, to be raised over seven years. The top of the range was considered a "stretch," given Spelman's identified pool of prospective donors and past fundraising history, but the college chose to go for the higher number. The decision was bold, especially considering that Spelman could not have anticipated some historic gifts that were about to come its way, pushing the campaign total ahead faster and making national headlines (Brooks, 2021).

At the outset of the campaign, Brooks was concerned about two questions. Did Spelman have a sufficient number of qualified donor prospects to support a $250 million goal and was the advancement office prepared to manage the campaign? With the advice and guidance of the campaign consulting firm

CCS, he intensified efforts to identify prospective donors and expanded the office, adding gift officers, stewardship specialists, and advancement services staff. He created a designated professional staff to help manage the campaign, led by Nelson Thomas, assistant vice president for development operations, and Keisha Leverette as campaign director. A Spelman alumna, Leverette had previous experience as a campaign manager, having directed a campaign for the Community Foundation of Baltimore, in Maryland (Brooks, 2021).

VOLUNTEER LEADERSHIP

Campbell and Brooks enlisted a volunteer executive committee to lead the campaign. The committee would be chaired by alumna Rosalind G. Brewer, who is also chair of the Spelman board of trustees. Brewer is chief executive officer of Walgreens Boots Alliance, having previously been president and CEO of Sam's Club, the first African American woman to lead a Walmart division. Two additional trustees, Gwendolyn Adams Norton and Ronda E. Stryker, were enlisted to serve as the committee's vice chairs. Notably, in view of Spelman's early support from John D. Rockefeller, the campaign executive committee also included Valerie B. Rockefeller, Chair of the Board of Trustees of the Rockefeller Brothers Fund.

The executive committee is far from ceremonial. Its members play an active role in all aspects of the campaign, going beyond policy and advice to participation in the identification, engagement, and solicitation of donors (Brooks, 2021).

A VIRTUAL KICKOFF

Spelman Ascends was announced with the news that it already had attained *96 percent* of its $250 million goal. With more than three years remaining, achievement of the dollar goal was all but assured.

The centerpiece of the virtual kickoff was a 44-minute video, featuring entertainment and testimonials from prominent Spelman students, alumnae, trustees, and donors. It culminated with remarks from campaign chair Brewer and President Campbell, who spoke to the strategic goals the campaign would help advance and its importance to the college's future. The president announced the campaign goal and substantial nucleus fund already achieved, emphasizing the point that the campaign would continue to 2024 (Spelman College, 2021).

LEADERSHIP GIFTS

The campaign's substantial nucleus fund encompassed major and principal gifts from Spelman trustees and commitments from long-standing corporate and foundation partners, including the Coca-Cola Foundation, Morgan Stanley, Ernst & Young Foundation, Goldman Sachs, and the Alfred P. Sloan Foundation. These gifts and three others made national headlines.

Ronda Stryker, a director of the medical equipment company Stryker Corporation, had been a member of Spelman's board since 1997. Her spouse, William Johnston, chairs investment bank Greenleaf Trust. Stryker and Johnston committed $30 million toward building the college's new Center for Innovation & the Arts, which would be Spelman's first new academic facility since the 1990s. The Stryker family had made significant gifts to Spelman in the past, but the new campaign commitment would set a record, ranking as the largest gift in the college's history at the time.

Spelman has long been known for its strengths in the arts. Providing its students with expertise in technology was among the goals articulated by President Campbell at her inauguration and was also a major theme in the college's strategic plan. The new center supported by the Stryker/Johnston gift would integrate the arts and technology by exploring technology-based solutions for urban problems; creating an entrepreneurship incubator for students; and helping to link Spelman to its community (Spelman College, 2018b).

The national media in 2020 reported that Reed Hastings, the co-founder and CEO of Netflix, and his spouse, Patty Quillin, would give $40 million each to the United Negro College Fund, Morehouse College, and Spelman College. "Generally, white capital flows to predominantly white institutions, perpetuating capital isolation," Hastings explained. Noting that HBCUs have smaller endowments than Ivy League institutions, Hasting said, "I think white people in our nation need to accept that it's a collective responsibility [to change that situation]." Hastings identified the murder of George Floyd in 2020 and the outpouring of emotion that followed as "the straw that broke the camel's back [in influencing] the size of the donation" (Sorkin, 2020).

The Hastings/Quillin gift to Spelman would support a scholarship fund named for alumna Dovey Johnson Roundtree, a civil rights leader and attorney who had helped to end the legal concept of "separate but equal." After graduating from Spelman, Roundtree became one of the first women to enter the Women's Army Military Corps during World War II and later became one of the first Black officers. After her Army service, she went to the Howard University Law School and later argued a case before the Interstate Commerce Commission that led to the desegregation of interstate bus travel in the United States (Spelman College, 2020b).

The Dovey Johnson Roundtree Fund would provide 20 first-year students with full scholarships annually for a decade. As President Campbell noted, "[The gift means that] at the end of 10 years we will have educated 200 students who will graduate debt free" (Spelman College, 2020c).

Author and philanthropist MacKenzie Scott rocked the philanthropy world in 2020 with the announcement that she had given more than $800 million to colleges serving "historically marginalized and underserved people" (Redden, 2021). Spelman received $20 million and—uncommonly for a gift of such magnitude—the money was totally unrestricted; it could be used to further the college's strategic objectives at the institution's discretion.

Scott explained the motivation for her gifts, saying "Like many, I watched the first half of 2020 with a mixture of heartbreak and horror. Life will never stop finding fresh ways to expose inequities in our systems; or waking us up to the fact that a civilization this imbalanced is not only unjust, but also unstable. What fills me with hope is the thought of what will come if each of us reflects on what we can offer. Opportunities that flowed from the mere chance of skin color, sexual orientation, gender, or zip code may have yielded resources that can be powerful levers for change" (Spelman College, 2020d).

CAMPAIGN PRIORITIES

As summarized in Table 8.1, objectives of Spelman Ascends are organized under four pillars, consistent with the college's strategic plan. By its announcement in 2021, the campaign already had helped launch new academic programs, including the Atlanta University Center for Art History and Curatorial Studies Collective; the Center for Black Entrepreneurship (in collaboration with Morehouse College and the Black Economic Alliance); and the Institute for the Study of Gender and Sexuality. Campaign funds also had supported Spelman's participation in the AUC Data Science Initiative, a collaboration with Morehouse, Clark Atlanta University, and Morehouse School of Medicine (Spelman College, n.d.-b).

Campaign priorities encompassed substantial facilities projects. The new Center for Innovation & the Arts, supported by the Stryker/Johnston gift, would bring together all of Spelman's arts programs in one place and would serve as a "front porch" for the college, including a second gallery for the Museum of Fine Art, a dance performance studio, and a high-tech digital black box theater. The facility also would include an Innovation Lab and the Hive, a double-height atrium including offices, a conference and event center, and a roof terrace. The campaign also would help fund renovation of the Rockefeller Fine Arts Building, which houses the Baldwin Burroughs Theater (Spelman College, n.d.-b).

CHALLENGES AND OPPORTUNITIES

Announcing a campaign with 96 percent of the goal already having been achieved–and three years left to run in the public phase—was an unusual decision. As Jessie Brooks (2021) explains, the goal had already been set before the exceptional lead gifts from Reed Hastings and Patty Quillin and from MacKenzie Scott had been received. Since both gifts were part of a larger amount distributed among a group of HBCUs, they could not have been anticipated at the time Spelman's campaign was in planning.

Those gifts pushed the nucleus fund total higher and faster than had been expected, but the $250 million campaign goal always had been a stretch and the balance of the campaign total would need to come from smaller gifts over the remaining years. For those reasons, the college decided to leave the goal and deadline unchanged and to focus its efforts on completing the campaign and meeting remaining needs. With achievement of the overall goal highly likely, the public phase could focus on some long-term priorities (Brooks, 2021).

Reflecting Gasman's (2010) observation about the historically low participation by HBCU alumni, mentioned previously, one priority for Spelman would be to increase alumnae participation in the annual fund, called "Spelman Strong." Having hovered around 32 percent at the beginning of the campaign, the participation rate decreased slightly to 28 percent and then

Table 8.1. Spelman College. Spelman Ascends-A Campaign for Spelman College: Campaign Priorities

Strategic priority	Objectives
Deliver the Spelman Promise	• Enhance scholarship support • Create a summer bridge program • Leading engines of social mobility. In an era when technology touches every aspect of our lives, Spelman graduates more Black women who complete PhDs in STEM
Elevate the Spelman Difference	• Fund endowed professorships • Fund faculty research and scholarly output
Enhance Operational Excellence	• Create a Technology Innovation Fund • Increase annual giving • Fund ongoing professional development
Promote Academic Innovation	• Build the Center for Innovation & the Arts • Renovate Rockefeller Fine Arts • Create Endowment for the Center • Enrich Spelman College Museum of Fine Art • Promote Academic Innovation

Source: Spelman College. n.d.-b. Spelman Ascends - A Campaign for Spelman College. https://www.spelman.edu/giving/spelman-ascends/spelman-ascends-overview (accessed May 10, 2021).

increased to 33 percent by 2020, against a goal of 40 percent by the end of the Spelman Ascends campaign (Brooks, 2021).

Another priority—during the campaign and after—would be to significantly increase Spelman's endowment, which stood at $453 million in 2021. Despite Spelman's high academic reputation and ranking, the fact remained that 48 percent of its students qualified for Pell grants based on their family income, and the college's tuition of about $43,000 remained a barrier for many. Increasing the amount available for scholarships, both through annual giving and endowment, would be a top priority for Spelman fundraising in the remainder of the campaign and beyond (Brooks, 2021).

As Reed Hastings noted, Spelman is similar to all HBCUs in having an endowment less than that of other institutions of comparable quality, reflecting the historic lack of wealth in the Black community and discrimination. But Brooks (2021) is optimistic, pointing to Spelman's case for support based on its demonstrated outcomes—its high graduation rate and the success of its alumnae in emerging fields.

Like all colleges and universities, Spelman faced challenges from the Covid-19 pandemic that began in 2020, forcing many events and donor visits to adopt a virtual format and complicating the work of advancement services. Routine back-office operations, such as acknowledging gifts, updating records, and maintaining stewardship activities, became challenging in the work-from-home and virtual environment. Brooks credits Spelman's advancement staff for having been "flexible and nimble" in response (Brooks, 2021).

LESSONS LEARNED AND LOOKING TO THE FUTURE

In 2021, with three years yet to run in Spelman Ascends, Jessie Brooks also was looking beyond its conclusion. The campaign had brought many new donors to Spelman and retaining their engagement would need to be a priority. There would be a renewed focus on donor stewardship and alumnae engagement programs. As the pandemic started to recede in 2021, Brooks was anticipating a future that would include more in-person contacts and events, recognizing that virtual events would likely remain a part of the mix. He noted in particular the stewardship events that have worked so well for Spelman—donor visits to the campus that include meetings with students. While virtual events might continue to provide such opportunities to donors unable to visit the campus, Brooks was certain that there could be no ongoing substitute for the in-person campus experience (Brooks, 2021).

The need for increased endowment also would be addressed in part through an enhanced planned giving program. Spelman began working with outside marketing consultants and added a planned giving specialist to the advancement office staff. Brooks (2021) was confident that the intense loyalty and close bonds of Spelman alumnae would provide a promising environment for planned giving in the years ahead.

Would there be future campaigns? Brooks acknowledges that some donors to Spelman's campaign, notably Hastings/Quillin and Scott, were motivated by their commitment to a cause rather than responding to the campaign. But he notes that such gifts are not the norm and argues that comprehensive campaigns bring important benefits. However, he notes, "It is our goal that these gifts *do* become the norm because of our impact and success in achieving outcomes" (Brooks, 2021).

Brooks emphasizes the importance of institutional strategic planning and views campaigns as essential for implementing institutional goals. And, he emphasizes, there are non-monetary benefits of campaigns; they help create excitement and momentum and advance the institution's reputation and brand. As he reflects on the benefits of Spelman Ascends in its successful fourth year, Brooks (2021) explains, "This campaign has significantly raised our visibility, both nationally and globally."

REFERENCES

Brooks, Jessie. 2021. Interview with author, June 1, 2021.

Campbell, Mary Schmidt. 2016. Equality: The Inaugural Address, April 9. https://www.spelman.edu/docs/presidents-office/2016-inaugural-address.pdf?sfvrsn=d6499150_6 (accessed May 8, 2021).

Connley, Courtney. 2015. "Mary Schmidt Campbell Named President of Spelman College." *Black Enterprise*, March 30. https://www.blackenterprise.com/mary-schmidt-campbell-named-president-spelman-college/ (accessed May 7, 2021).

Gasman, Mary Beth. 2010. "Introduction to special issue: Fundraising and Philanthropy within the Historically Black College and University Setting." *International Journal of Educational Advancement* (10), December 22, 123–125.

Lefever, Harry G. 2005. *Undaunted by the Fight: Spelman College and the Civil Rights Movement, 1957-1967*. Macon, GA: Mercer University Press.

McAllister-Grande, Brian. 2015. *The Campaign for Spelman College*. Cambridge, MA: Harvard Educational Press.

Peeples, Yarbrah. 2010. "Philanthropy and the curriculum: The role of philanthropy in the development of curriculum at Spelman College." *International Journal of Educational Advancement* (10), December 22, 245–260.

Redden, Elizabeth. 2021. "A Fairy Godmother for Once-Overlooked Colleges." *Inside Higher Ed*, January 4. https://www.insidehighered.com/news/2021/01/04/mackenzie-scott-surprises-hbcus-tribal-colleges-and-community-colleges-multimillion#:~:text=A%20Fairy%20Godmother%20for%20Once,those%20 from%20low%2Dincome%20backgrounds (accessed May 10, 2021).

Sorkin, Andrew Ross. 2020. "Netflix C.E.O. Reed Hastings Gives $120 Million to Historically Black Colleges." *New York Times*, June 17. https://www.nytimes.com/2020/06/17/business/netflix-reed-hastings-hbcus.html (accessed June 2, 2021).

Spelman College. n.d.-a. About. https://www.spelman.edu/about-us (accessed May 7, 2021).

Spelman College. n.d.-b. Spelman Ascends - A Campaign for Spelman College. https://www.spelman.edu/giving/spelman-ascends/spelman-ascends-overview (accessed May 10, 2021).

Spelman College. 2014. "Spelman College Exceeds Fundraising Goal; Prepares for Next Era of Leadership." Press release, n.d. https://www.spelman.edu/about-us/news-and-events/news-releases/2014/07/09/spelman-college-campaign-results (accessed May 7, 2021).

Spelman College. 2018a. "Excellence in Education: Top Rankings and Honors Reveal Spelman College's Academic Edge." Press release, February 2. https://www.spelman.edu/about-us/news-and-events/news-releases/2018/02/02/excellence-in-education-reveal-spelman-college-academic-edge.

Spelman College. 2018b. "Spelman College Receives $30 Million Gift from Trustee Ronda Stryker and Spouse, William Johnston, to Support New Center for Innovation & the Arts." Press release, December 13. https://www.spelman.edu/about-us/news-and-events/news-releases/2018/12/13/spelman-receives-30-million-gift-from-ronda-stryker-and-william-johnston (accessed May 10, 2021).

Spelman College. 2020a. *History and Traditions: 2020 Reference Guide.* https://www.spelman.edu/docs/alumnae-affairs/spelman-history-traditions-brochure.pdf?sfvrsn=eda80791_26 (accessed May 18, 2021).

Spelman College. 2020b. "Patty Quillin and Reed Hastings Fund 200 Full Scholarships at Spelman College with a $40 Million Gift." Press release, June 17. https://www.prnewswire.com/news-releases/patty-quillin-and-reed-hastings-fund-200-full-scholarships-at-spelman-college-with-a-40-million-gift-301078698.html (accessed May 10, 2021).

Spelman College. 2020c. "Spelman Announces Inaugural Recipients of the Dovey Johnson Roundtree, C'38, Presidential Scholarship." Press release, July 22. https://www.spelman.edu/about-us/news-and-events/news-releases/2020/07/22/spelman-announces-inaugural-recipients-of-the-dovey-johnson-roundtree-c-38-presidential-scholarship (accessed June 2, 2021).

Spelman College. 2020d. "Magnanimous Gift from MacKenzie Scott Bolsters Spelman College's Strategic Outcomes." Press release, July 28. https://www.spelman.edu/about-us/news-and-events/news-releases/2020/07/28/magnanimous-gift-from-mackenzie-scott-bolsters-spelman-college-s-strategic-outcomes (accessed May 10, 2021).

Spelman College. 2021. Campaign Launch Announcement. https://www.spelman.edu/giving/spelman-ascends/spelman-ascends-overview (accessed May 10, 2021).

PART IV

Associate's Colleges

The Carnegie Classification of Institutions of Higher Education identifies some institutions as Baccalaureate/Associate's Colleges; they do award bachelor's degrees, but most of the degrees that they award are two-year associate's degrees. The category of Associate's Colleges includes those that award only two-year degrees. The latter are divided into nine sub-categories based on their disciplinary focus (transfer, career, and technical or mixed) and type of students they serve (traditional, nontraditional, or mixed). Most institutions in this category are public community colleges.

Until recent years, community colleges have not maintained fundraising programs on the scale of four-year colleges and universities. But reductions in public funding and the growing emphasis on educational access and affordability have led some to increase their investment in fundraising and to launch campaigns (Brookey, 2019).

Historically, most gifts to community colleges have come from local business and industry and have been designated to support specific programs of interest to the donor company. As Smith and colleagues (2017, p. 16) describe, companies were "essentially sponsoring job-training programs." Community colleges have faced significant challenges in fundraising from individual donors. Many of their students attend part time and only attend for two years, not forming the same emotional attachment as students at residential four-year colleges. And community college graduates who go on to complete bachelor's degrees at four-year institutions are likely to have divided loyalties and interests (Smith et al., 2017).

However, as one branding expert observes, community colleges are well-positioned to build a case for support, based both on reason and emotion. Many community college students come from low-income backgrounds; gifts that help them complete their educations can have a significant impact on their lives. The institution can tell stories of lives transformed, going beyond institutional needs and putting a human face on their campaigns. And meeting the needs of local businesses for trained employees can have an impact on economic and community development beyond those firms. In other words, gifts to community colleges can offer a substantial return-on-investment (Zekovic, 2020).

Indeed, in 2021, MacKenzie Scott announced gifts totaling $2.73 billion to colleges and advocacy nonprofits focused on broadening access to higher education, some of which included community colleges (Whitford, 2021). Some saw Scott's gifts as a potential turning point for community college philanthropy. As Amir Pasic, dean of the Indiana University Lilly Family School of Philanthropy, observed, "It [Scott's gift] bestows a kind of symbolic recognition of the worth and the importance and the value of these institutions in our society" (Whitford, 2021).

CENTRAL PIEDMONT COMMUNITY COLLEGE

This section of the book includes one case study, Central Piedmont Community College in Charlotte, North Carolina. While other community colleges have enjoyed fundraising success, Central Piedmont is unusual in having conducted three successful comprehensive campaigns, including one announced in 2019 with a $40 million goal, which is the subject of the case study. The college also has received a significant number of principal and major gifts from corporations and individuals. Its success reflects the philanthropic culture of its home community and the emphasis that long-serving presidents at Central Piedmont have given to their fundraising roles. The campaign also followed an academic study that ranked Charlotte low on the basis of the economic mobility of its residents. Community leaders responded with a plan to address the problem, including strategies that corresponded with Central Piedmont's mission and strategic plan.

REFERENCES

Brookey, Lauren F. 2019. "Raising Funds for Community Colleges." In *Advancing Higher Education: New Strategies for Fundraising, Philanthropy, and Engagement*, edited by Michael J. Worth and Matthew T. Lambert. Lanham, MD: Rowman & Littlefield, 211–218.

Smith, Everett A., Michael T. Miller, and G. David Gearhart. 2017. "Using Feasibility Studies in Capital Fundraising Campaigns: A National Survey of Community

Colleges." *Journal of Applied Research in the Community College*, 24 (2), Fall, 15–27.
Whitford, Emma. 2021. "Gifts That Keep Giving." *Inside Higher Education*, June 16. https://www.insidehighered.com/news/2021/06/16/mackenzie-scott-gifts-millions-community-colleges-regional-colleges-and-nonprofits (accessed June 30, 2021).
Zekovic, Meliha. 2020. "Capital Campaigns for Community Colleges: Making the Case to Donors." ĒLLIANCE, April 15. https://aha.elliance.com/2020/04/15/capital-campaigns-for-community-colleges/ (accessed May 18, 2021).

Chapter 9

Central Piedmont Community College

POWERING A STRONGER FUTURE

Central Piedmont Community College serves Mecklenburg County, North Carolina, which includes the city of Charlotte. Charlotte is the largest metropolitan region in the state and a major financial center, including the corporate headquarters of Bank of America and Truist Financial, among others. It is also the fastest growing metropolitan area in the nation, having added over 44,000 people in 2020 alone (Which Local Counties, 2021).

The college was founded in 1963, when the North Carolina General Assembly passed the state community college bill, and is governed by a Board of Trustees. Trustees are appointed by other public entities, including the Governor of North Carolina. Having begun with 1,600 students on a single campus, Central Piedmont is one of the largest community colleges in North Carolina, encompassing six campuses and two centers and enrolling about 43,000 students annually (Central Piedmont Community College, 2021a).

The college offers associate's degrees in various fields and maintains articulation agreements with four-year institutions, enabling graduates to transfer into baccalaureate degree programs. It also offers various continuing education programs and a variety of career-oriented programs, some of which lead to professional certification or licensure (Central Piedmont Community College, 2021b). Central Piedmont notes that its alumni include a Pulitzer Prize winner, a Metropolitan Opera star, an Olympic gold medalist, a Congressional Medal of Honor winner, a television actress, and a pro football player—in addition to many others who are leaders in various trades and professions (Central Piedmont Community College, 2021a).

ADVANCEMENT AT CENTRAL PIEDMONT

Central Piedmont has enjoyed continuity in its advancement leadership. Kevin McCarthy served as the college's chief advancement officer starting in 2004 and was named vice president for institutional advancement in 2012. In 2020, he was named executive vice president for institutional advancement, having also held responsibility for other administrative offices at the college during various leadership transitions.

McCarthy's responsibilities include development and alumni relations; a separate communications office reports directly to the president. McCarthy also manages the college's foundation, with assets of about $70 million (McCarthy, 2021).

HISTORY OF PREVIOUS CAMPAIGNS

Central Piedmont is unusual among community colleges in having a history of successful previous campaigns. The college completed a campaign in 2007, which raised $28 million. In 2009, it launched "Legacy & Promise," a $30 million campaign that concluded on the college's 50th anniversary in 2013 (Thomas, 2012). That campaign raised $34 million in cash, exceeding its goal, and received an additional $30 million in in-kind gifts, including equipment given to support a new technology building (Central Piedmont Community College Foundation, 2015). Kevin McCarthy directed both of the previous campaigns as well as the campaign discussed in this case study.

McCarthy attributes Central Piedmont's history of campaign success to the economy and philanthropic culture of Charlotte, to the college's wide footprint and impact across the region, and to the leadership of the college's presidents over the years. In addition to hosting multiple corporate headquarters, Charlotte has a long tradition of giving by local families focused on strengthening the community. Formal campaigns are a familiar model in Charlotte. As McCarthy describes, a campaign is a "known way of doing business" and the local donor community responds, often to multiple simultaneous campaigns by local colleges, universities, and nonprofit organizations.

McCarthy (2021) observes that Central Piedmont's recent presidents have viewed engagement with the community's leaders and fundraising as central aspects of their role, perhaps to a greater extent than most community college presidents. He also notes that unlike many community colleges, where presidential turnover is typically high, Central Piedmont has enjoyed significant continuity in its leadership.

The college's founding president, Richard Hagemeyer, served for twenty-three years, until 1986, and was credited with much of the college's early growth. Ruth Shaw, the college's second president, laid the groundwork for the expansion to multiple campuses in the county and developed strong relationships with business and industry partners. Former president Tony Zeiss served for twenty-four years and led two campaigns. Kandi Deitemeyer, appointed as Zeiss's successor in 2017, was only the fourth president in the college's history of nearly 60 years. The presidents' long tenures and involvement in the continuity have developed strong relationships with business and community leaders, who have responded to the college's multiple campaigns (McCarthy, 2021).

A TRANSFORMATIONAL MOMENT

An academic study published in 2014 became a "transformational moment" for Charlotte, causing community leaders to reflect and reorder their priorities (McCarthy, 2021). Conducted by scholars Raj Chetty, Nathaniel Hendren, Patrick Kline, and Emmanuel Saez, the study ranked U.S. cities in terms of the social mobility of their residents (Chetty et al., 2014). Charlotte was ranked 50th among the fifty cities studied. The finding was a shock to the leaders of the community and called forth an immediate response (McCarthy, 2021).

A Charlotte-Mecklenburg Opportunity Task Force was formed, including Central Piedmont's president as well as other community and business leaders. The task force worked during 2015 and 2016 and focused "on the inheritance of intergenerational poverty and its negative impact on the life trajectory of far too many of Charlotte-Mecklenburg's children and youth" (Leading on Opportunity, 2021). The task force developed strategies for action, including an emphasis on early care and education; college and career readiness; and child and family stability (Leading on Opportunity, 2021).

Among educational strategies identified by the task force were: "Equip our students with the skills and education they will need to build and support thriving families; Broaden the range of and access to high quality college and career pathways offered by our K-12 and postsecondary institutions; Expand and strengthen support for first-generation and other low-socioeconomic students who need help transitioning to and completing postsecondary education"; and "Elevate and actively promote the critical importance of acquiring a postsecondary degree and/or industry certification for our young people to successfully compete in our rapidly changing, technologically advanced labor market" (Leading on Opportunity, 2021).

Charlotte's strategies for addressing a serious social problem had placed Central Piedmont's mission at the center of the community's agenda. It was in this context that Kandi Deitemeyer arrived as Central Piedmont's president in 2017.

INTENTIONAL, TRANSFORMATIONAL, IMPACTING STUDENTS, AND COMMUNITY

Deitemeyer was an experienced community college leader. She had graduated from Polk Community College in Florida and earned her baccalaureate, master's, and doctoral degrees at the University of South Florida. She began her administrative career at Polk and then moved on through a series of administrative positions at other community colleges. She was president of the College of The Albemarle, in North Carolina, prior to her appointment at Central Piedmont in 2017 (Belk Center, 2021).

Soon after her arrival at Central Piedmont, Deitemeyer conducted a survey of employees to gain their views on the college's future. She also engaged consultants to help gather data on the college's position and programs. A self-assessment looked at ways to improve student-success initiatives. Another study focused on the use of human, financial, and facilities resources and a marketing study obtained opinions and insights from a variety of internal and external constituencies. These studies provided data for a new strategic planning committee. Supported by the consulting firm Paulien and Associates, the committee led an inclusive planning process that culminated in a plan presented to the college community in 2019 (Central Piedmont Community College, n.d.-a).

The new plan clarified the college's mission, vision, and values and established five strategic goals: Creating a Unified and Focused Vision for Student Success; Promoting Academic Excellence through Community Engagement and Partnerships; Advancing Our Organizational Culture; Making Equity a Priority; and Telling Our Story. Specific objectives were articulated under each of those five goals.

Objectives identified under Telling Our Story included branding and communications initiatives as well as "leveraging supporters." Increased philanthropy had become a strategic priority of the college, setting the stage for Central Piedmont's next campaign (Central Piedmont Community College, n.d.-a).

POWERING A STRONGER FUTURE

The new campaign began quietly in 2018 and was announced at a major event in the fall, 2019. The goal was $40 million and $23.5 million had been committed during the quiet phase. The kickoff included remarks by the campaign's volunteer leaders and President Deitemeyer, who stated the case for support in terms of the campaign's social and community impact.

Echoing the report of the Opportunity Task Force, Deitemeyer said, "For those who want our community to thrive and want to make an investment, education is a game changer. Central Piedmont is a great place to help students thrive and be successful in our community. I think there is no better investment for Mecklenburg [County's] future" (Central Piedmont Community College, 2019).

CAMPAIGN PRIORITIES

As summarized in Table 9.1, campaign priorities are based on five pillars, which reflect the college's strategic plan and its emphasis on student impact: $15 million to fund student scholarships and support the student emergency fund; $9.5 million for student support services, such as academic and career advising, leadership opportunities, out-of-classroom experiences, enhanced disability services, and the Summer Bridge program that helps students prepare for their first semester of college; $9.5 million to further instructional excellence through support for programs, equipment, and other resources and faculty; $5 million for specific programs that foster economic mobility, such as the Accelerated Career Training program for under-and unemployed adults, the early childhood education program that trains pre-K teachers, and strategic workforce partnerships; and $1 million for the college's annual fund to respond to evolving priorities and needs.

LEADERSHIP GIFTS

Central Piedmont has received principal gifts at levels unusual for a community college, reflecting the history and traditions discussed previously. The campaign nucleus fund included a $9 million planned gift from an anonymous donor and a subsequent anonymous gift of $10 million was designated to enhance instruction and learning in the arts and humanities.

Additional principal and major gifts were announced at the kickoff event and over the following months of the campaign. Many came from local donors with a long history of philanthropy focused on the needs of Charlotte and Mecklenburg County. And the designated purposes of gifts reflected the emphasis on economic mobility that had become a central priority—for the community as well as Central Piedmont.

Table 9.1. Powering a Stronger Future: Campaign Priorities

Priorities	Objectives
Removing Financial Barriers and Expanding Access to Opportunities **Goal: $15 million**	Scholarships Student Emergency Fund
Supporting Student Success, Equity, and Engagement **Goal: $9.5 million**	Summer Bridge Academic and Career Advising and Mentoring Leadership Opportunities Out-of-Classroom Experiences Disability Services
Ensuring Instructional Excellence and Relevance **Goal: $9.5 million**	Faculty Support Center for Teaching and Learning New Program Development Strengthening & Expanding High Demand Programs Instructional Equipment and Resources
Fostering Economic Mobility and Responding to Community Needs **Goal $5 million**	Accelerated Career Training Early Childhood Education Strategic Workforce Partnerships
Responding to Present and Emerging Needs **Goal: $1 million**	Central Piedmont Annual Fund

Source: Central Piedmont Community College. 2021d. *Powering A Stronger Future: The Campaign for Central Piedmont*. https://www.cpccfoundation.org/campaign/ (accessed May 28, 2021).

Wilton L. and Mary Parr had made previous major gifts to Central Piedmont and their names are recognized through naming one of the college's auditoriums as well as scholarship funds and faculty awards. Mr. Parr had graduated from Virginia Tech and subsequently retired as senior vice president for marketing at Piedmont Natural Gas. He completed courses at Central Piedmont after his retirement, while also tutoring adult students. In connection with the campaign, the Parrs committed a gift to establish the Wilton L. and Mary W. Parr Center for Teaching and Learning Excellence, to facilitate professional development of faculty (Central Piedmont College, n.d.-b).

The Dowd Foundation of Charlotte and Charlotte Pipe & Foundry committed $1 million for plumbing and pipefitting scholarships. The Dowd family founded Charlotte Pipe & Foundry in 1901 and the company had become the nation's leading manufacturer of cast iron and plastic pipe and fittings for plumbing applications (Central Piedmont College, n.d.-b).

The late C. D. Spangler was a highly successful businessman based in Charlotte, who also had served as president of the University of North Carolina. The C. D. Spangler Foundation committed a gift of $1 million to Central Piedmont's campaign, to support the college's early childhood education program (Central Piedmont College, n.d.-b).

Prominent Charlotte real estate investors Peggy and Bob Culbertson gave $1 million to establish the 49erNext scholarship program, a co-admission transfer partnership program between Central Piedmont and the University of North Carolina Charlotte (Justin, 2019).

The Gambrell Foundation, a long-time philanthropic presence in Charlotte, associated with the Belk department store family, committed $1 million to establish the Gambrell Opportunity Scholarships to support high school graduates from low-income backgrounds to complete their associate's degrees. The Foundation also committed $875,000 to provide laptop computers to low-income students (Benz, 2018).

The Leon Levine Foundation of Charlotte, established by the founder of Family Dollar stores, made a commitment to name the college's new health sciences facility the Leon Levine Health Sciences Center (McCarthy, 2021).

The Dickson Foundation of Charlotte made a commitment to assist the college in creating a licensed practical nursing program to address regional workforce needs and create career opportunities for students (McCarthy, 2021).

As mentioned previously, Charlotte is a major financial center and financial institutions supported the Central Piedmont campaign. Locally headquartered Bank of America committed $1 million for a jobs initiative to help "students of color successfully complete the education and training necessary to enter the workforce and embark on a path to success in the Charlotte region" (Central Piedmont Community College, 2020a). Wells Fargo, with a significant presence in Charlotte, made a grant commitment to expand services for minority-owned small businesses in the region. And JPMorgan Chase, with a growing presence in the region, made a series of grants to support training in technical fields (McCarthy, 2021).

CAMPAIGN PLANNING AND STRATEGIES

As Kevin McCarthy began planning for the new campaign in 2017, he was able to draw on his own experience in directing two previous campaigns for Central Piedmont. Given his long experience with Central Piedmont and its two previous campaigns, McCarthy had a good sense of what would be a challenging but realistic goal. He also knew the community and had a good sense of where support might be forthcoming. Rather than hire a consultant, the college's president and staff "did their own feasibility study," meeting with individuals in the community and focusing on leadership gifts (McCarthy, 2021).

ENGAGED VOLUNTEER LEADERSHIP

McCarthy also recognized that budget resources available to support the campaign would be limited. The advancement staff would remain small and still would need to manage the college's ongoing special events and other programs in addition to the added challenge of a campaign. Like most community colleges, Central Piedmont did not have an extensive network of alumni donors. That would require looking to the local community for major gifts, and contacts established through volunteers would be essential (McCarthy, 2021). Given these realities, the campaign would need to be volunteer-driven.

Steps already had been taken to expand the foundation board. Over the past 15 years, the board had been increased from 12 to more than 30 members, including individuals who added broad knowledge of the community and its philanthropic resources. A campaign committee of 13 members was created. It included three co-chairs: Weston M. Andress, regional president of PNC Bank; marketing executive Linda Lockman-Brooks; and J. Carlton Showalter Jr., a prominent builder. Patricia A. Rodgers was enlisted as honorary chair of the campaign. Rodgers is a Central Piedmont alumna, president and CEO of Rodgers Builders, and chair of the college's foundation board. She and her late husband, B.D. Rodgers, had served as co-chairs of the college's previous campaign (Central Piedmont Community College, 2021d). As McCarthy (2021) describes, the volunteer leaders are highly motivated and engaged in all aspects of the campaign, including the identification of donor prospects and solicitation visits.

CHALLENGES AND OPPORTUNITIES

As Kevin McCarthy (2021) describes, many of the fundraising strategies practiced by Central Piedmont during the campaign are not necessarily unusual in the larger higher education context, but their application in a community college might be considered innovative. In essence, Central Piedmont was ahead of the curve in adopting some traditional practices within its sector and the benefits came to be realized during the Powering a Stronger Future campaign.

That included a well-established planned giving program, led by a part-time planned giving officer who had been associated with the college for 25 years, working with a committee of the foundation board that includes local estate-planning attorneys. Although the campaign did not count revocable planned gift intentions, realized bequests had an impact, including the $9 million gift that was mentioned previously (McCarthy, 2021).

Central Piedmont's campaign faced the headwinds of the Covid-19 pandemic in 2020 and 2021 and adapted by shifting to virtual events. Having a president who was still early in her tenure was a plus, since the opportunity to meet her provided an incentive for some who participated in those events (McCarthy, 2021). Like other institutions, the college created an emergency fund to assist students who were impacted by the pandemic and an anonymous donor pledged $100,000 to match gifts to the fund (Central Piedmont College, 2020b).

LESSONS LEARNED AND LOOKING TO THE FUTURE

By mid-2021, McCarthy was anticipating that Powering a Stronger Future would soon attain its $40 million goal. The campaign nevertheless would continue through its planned end date in 2022, likely exceeding its goal by a significant margin. McCarthy already was looking beyond 2022 at strategies to strengthen the ongoing fundraising program post-campaign. Charlotte's continued economic growth and the community's focus on economic mobility would place the college in a favorable environment. But there was a need to address weaknesses in its fundraising position. That would include expanding the donor base and building the staff.

Despite the traditional challenges that community colleges face in gaining alumni support, expanding alumni engagement would be a high priority for the remainder of the campaign and after its conclusion. Powering a Stronger Future included the first six-figure gift from an alumnus in the college's history and McCarthy was optimistic that additional major gifts could be obtained with sustained alumni engagement in future years. He was planning to retain a consulting firm to assess the college's staffing and programs with an eye to possible growth, to include intensified efforts to promote annual and planned giving (McCarthy, 2021).

While acknowledging that campaigns may not be the right strategy for all institutions at all times, McCarthy (2021) points to their distinctive benefits. A campaign forces an institution to identify its priorities and clarify its messages. And the campaign provides a platform for communication and outreach. Will there be a next campaign for Central Piedmont Community College? McCarthy is confident that there will be and that the goal will exceed the total achieved by Powering a Stronger Future.

REFERENCES

Belk Center for Community College Leadership and Research/North Carolina State University. 2021. *Kandi W. Deitemeyer, Ed.D.* https://belk-center.ced.ncsu.edu/what-we-do/our-advisory-board/dr-kandi-deitemeyer/ (accessed May 26, 2021).

Benz, Mallory. 2018. *Central Piedmont Today*, November 13. https://blogs.cpcc.edu/cpcctoday/2018/11/13/gambrell-foundation-grant-will-provide-central-piedmont-students-pathway-to-economic-mobility/ (accessed June 22, 2021).

Central Piedmont Community College. n.d.-a. Strategic plan. https://en.calameo.com/read/000876273fabc7e685d8e (accessed May 26, 2021).

Central Piedmont Community College. n.d.-b. *Annual Report 2019-2020*. https://en.calameo.com/read/00087627311eff0fc4583b (accessed June 7, 2021).

Central Piedmont Community College. 2019. "Central Piedmont Announces Campaign Goal of $40 Million." Press release, October 31. https://www.cpcc.edu/news/central-piedmont-announces-campaign-goal-40-million (accessed June 4, 2021).

Central Piedmont Community College. 2020a. "Bank of America Commits $1 Million to College for Jobs Initiative." Press release, November 19. https://www.cpcc.edu/news/bank-america-commits-1-million-college-jobs-initiative (accessed June 22, 2021).

Central Piedmont Community College. 2020b. "Anonymous Donor Gives to College's Emergency Fund, Issues Matching-Gift Challenge." Press release, March 30. https://www.cpcc.edu/news/anonymous-donor-gives-colleges-emergency-fund-issues-matching-gift-challenge (accessed June 26, 2021).

Central Piedmont Community College. 2021a. College History. https://www.cpcc.edu/about-central-piedmont/college-history (accessed May 26, 2021).

Central Piedmont Community College. 2021b. Academics. https://www.cpcc.edu/academics (accessed May 26, 2021).

Central Piedmont Community College. 2021d. Powering A Stronger Future: The Campaign for Central Piedmont. Website. https://www.cpccfoundation.org/campaign/ (accessed May 28, 2021).

Central Piedmont Community College Foundation. 2015. Website. https://www.cpccfoundation.org/blog/category/alumni/?page=18 (accessed May 28, 2021).

Chetty, Raj, Nathaniel Hendren, Patrick Kline, and Emmanuel Saez. 2014. "Where Is the Land of Opportunity? The Geography of Intergenerational Mobility in the United States." *Quarterly Journal of Economics*, 129 (4) June, 1553–1623.

Justin, Josephine. 2019. "UNC Charlotte and CPCC Partner for the 49erNext Program." *Ninertimes*, October 22. https://www.ninertimes.com/news/unc-charlotte-and-cpcc-partner-for-the-49ernext-program/article_61460884-ed2a-11e9-ad89-bb68791e266a.html (accessed June 12, 2021).

Leading on Opportunity. 2021. *Our Children. Their Future. Our Commitment.* https://www.leadingonopportunity.org/report/executive-summary (accessed June 22, 2021).

McCarthy, Kevin. 2021. Interview with author, June 22, 2021.

Thomas, Jennifer. 2012. "Central Piedmont Community College Raises Bar for Fundraising." *Charlotte Business Journal*, February 2. https://www.bizjournals.com/charlotte/print-edition/2012/02/03/cpcc-raises-bar-for-fundraising.html (accessed May 26, 2021).

"Which Local Counties Are Leading Charlotte's Booming Growth? 2021." *Charlotte Business Journal*, May 7. https://www.wsoctv.com/news/local/which-local-counties-are-leading-charlottes-booming-growth/NZYIIGYW7FEHJJH3UTCQOEBVGM/ (accessed June 23, 2021).

Chapter 10

New Directions: The Years Ahead

The case studies of comprehensive campaigns discussed in the preceding chapters are drawn from a wide range of institutions, in different parts of the United States and at different points in their histories.

They include a relatively young private university in the Northeast campaigning to enhance its research standing; a distinguished private university in the South moving beyond near-destruction to pursue bold goals; a prestigious public university in the Mid-Atlantic aiming to sustain momentum in its third century; a public university in the Mid-West raising funds to enhance its own programs and bring economic rejuvenation to its region; a public university on the West Coast focused on the economic mobility of its diverse students and undertaking its first campaign; a unique liberal arts college with two campuses turning to philanthropy to implement an innovative new financial model; a distinguished historically Black college for women, located in the South, seeking resources to continue and increase its excellence; and a community college in the South raising funds to help address urgent economic and social priorities of the city and county that it serves. Their campaign goals ranged from $40 million to $5 billion!

What might be learned from these cases? A caveat is required. As explained in the Introduction to this book, the selection of institutions and campaigns was not random. These cases are not necessarily representative of all colleges and universities or campaigns. These case studies do not provide a basis for developing any theories about comprehensive campaigns. But they provide selected examples of how colleges and universities have adapted the campaign model to address their particular needs and circumstances and may suggest some new directions that will continue in the future.

TRADITIONAL PRINCIPLES WITH VARIATIONS

As many authors have observed, conditions in society, the economy, and higher education have changed significantly over the many decades since the campaign model was developed. However, the defining characteristics of traditional campaigns that were discussed in chapter 1 are, with variations, still observable in the case studies included in this book.

Goals and Deadlines

All of the campaigns had a public goal and, with the exception of Tulane, announced a specific deadline for achieving it. And all followed the usual sequence of phases—a planning phase, a quiet phase, and a public phase—with a high-visibility event to mark the transition from the quiet to the public phase.

There were some variations. The Rochester Institute of Technology (RIT) and the University of Virginia (UVA) counted gifts from the end of their previous campaigns. Youngstown State University (YSU) increased the goal of the campaign in its final year—and exceeded that higher target. Cal State LA and Central Piedmont Community College continued the campaign to its original closing date despite having exceeded the original goal ahead of schedule. Spelman College announced its campaign having already achieved 96 percent of its goal. RIT extended its campaign in light of challenges presented by the Covid-19 pandemic. UVA pre-announced the campaign and its goal a year before its formal kickoff, and RIT adopted the expansive counting policies of a blended campaign.

Specific practices differed, but in all cases, there were goals and deadlines—and counting policies—that were transparent.

Emphasis on Principal and Major Gifts

All of the campaigns emphasized principal and major gifts. Some chief advancement officers who were interviewed mentioned increasing alumni participation in annual giving as a priority, both during and following the campaign. Spelman College cited a specific target for giving participation, and Tulane set a goal for alumni engagement, a broader concept. But the excitement surrounded the large gifts that comprised a substantial portion of campaign totals and had the greatest impact on the institution and its programs.

In the traditional campaign model, solicitation proceeds from the top-rated prospects to lower levels (sequential fundraising). All of the institutions did announce significant gifts in connection with the campaign kickoff, consistent with the assumption that at least some donors may be influenced by what others already have given. But some also realized significant principal gifts later in the campaign, during the public phase, reflecting the extended length of campaigns and the time required to advance relationships with donors.

Some cases reveal creative strategies for leveraging leadership gifts, for example, RIT's use of donor funds to match state and corporate grants and St. John's success in increasing participation in response to a $50 million challenge.

Integration of Strategic Planning and Campaign

All of the institutions, with the exception of Tulane, had developed a strategic plan in advance of the campaign, and fundraising priorities generally tracked the themes of the plan. While Tulane did not adopt a formal institution-wide strategic plan, some of its academic units developed plans and the campaign closely reflected directions articulated by the president. St. John's new financial model may not meet the strict definition of a strategic plan, but it clearly represents a new strategy for the college. Six of the campaigns (RIT, Tulane, UVA, Cal State LA, Spelman College, Central Piedmont) summarize campaign priorities in terms of broad themes, or pillars, related to institutional strategies.

Volunteer Leadership

All of the campaigns enlisted volunteer leaders, but their roles varied. In some cases, the role of volunteers was limited—primarily lending visibility and credibility to the campaign. In other cases, volunteers played more central roles, including involvement in at least some solicitations. Only Tulane established an extensive national volunteer structure and demonstrated an innovative approach by integrating the regional committees into the national leadership council. UVA did not implement a national volunteer structure, having found it to be an unrewarding role for volunteers in its previous campaign. Only Central Piedmont's campaign could be described as volunteer-driven, with volunteers primarily involved in donor contacts.

In sum, the cases in this book suggest that the defining campaign practices discussed in chapter 1 are still alive and well in today's comprehensive campaigns. But they have been adapted to meet the unique circumstances of specific colleges and universities as well as changes in the environment.

ADAPTING THE MODEL TO CHANGING REALITIES

Some people raise the question of whether the comprehensive campaign remains an effective strategy or whether it is a twentieth-century idea that is no longer relevant in a rapidly-changing, global, and networked society. It is worth considering the pros and cons of campaigns and ways in which the traditional model has been adapted to address some of the concerns.

All of the chief advancement officers who were interviewed for the case studies in this book offered the view that campaigns will continue to be a fundraising strategy—at their institutions and in higher education generally. Some unique benefits of campaigns that were mentioned include the following:

- Preparing for a campaign brings discipline to an institution's planning and messaging.
- Promotion of the campaign generates visibility for the institution. As Jessie Brooks, vice president at Spelman College, noted, "This campaign has significantly raised our visibility, both nationally and globally" (Brooks, 2021).
- The visibility of the campaign provides opportunities to also advance important institutional goals for communications, marketing, branding, and alumni engagement.
- Comprehensive campaigns encompass a wide range of institutional priorities, increasing the odds that some will coincide with those of donors.
- A campaign raises the visibility of philanthropy and may help build a culture of philanthropy, with long-term benefits.
- A campaign provides opportunities for volunteers, including members of the governing or foundation board, to become involved in a tangible way in helping advance the university they serve.
- A campaign may help strengthen institutional pride. As Janet Dial, vice president at Cal State LA, expressed it, "A campaign just gives a university an excuse to be louder and prouder" (Dial, 2021).

However, those who question the continued relevance of the campaign model typically raise three issues: changing donor motivations and behaviors; dynamic institutional needs; and changing definitions of community. It is worth considering these points and looking at how campaigns have evolved to address them.

New Donors

Some argue that the traditional campaign model reflects obsolete assumptions about giving. Many corporations and foundations are no longer responsive to campaigns and follow the concept of strategic philanthropy, supporting causes and organizations that align with their own goals and priorities. Some individual donors are becoming more like corporations and foundations in their thinking, also taking a strategic or entrepreneurial approach and preferring to support programs with measurable *impact* rather than the traditional campaign priorities of annual giving, endowment, and bricks-and-mortar projects. Referring specifically to principal gifts, consultant Karin George (2021) argues: "The bells and whistles of a campaign are not needed when you have the right messages, messengers, and donors. Donors don't give to campaigns, but to the priorities that drive them when you ask."

But "impact" involves some nuance and donor motivations are complex. For example, in one academic study, the top motivation among donors of mega gifts to colleges and universities was the desire to give back for the benefits they had received from their educations, suggesting some degree of institutional loyalty (Worth et al., 2020). This is reflected, for example, in Warren Winiarski's explanation of the $50 million gift that he and his spouse made to St. John's College, saying "My St. John's education enabled me to acquire the proficiency and skills I needed . . ." (St. John's College, 2021).

The desire to have impact also ranked high among donor motivations that were identified in the referenced study (Worth et al., 2020), but the definition of impact was differentiated. Some donors wished to have impact on the institution itself, helping to advance its standing or the quality of one of its programs. Others intended to have a positive impact on a specific community—a state, city, or region—often related to economic stability or growth. Others were focused on a cause, social change, or a political agenda and were supporting the institution as a *vehicle* for addressing it (Worth et al., 2020).

The widely publicized gifts from MacKenzie Scott and from Reed Hastings and Patty Quillin to HBCUs, discussed in the case of Spelman College, were intended to advance the cause of social justice. Those gifts were made to institutions the donors had not attended themselves but that demonstrated outcomes consistent with their social goals. Other gifts mentioned in case studies, for example to Central Piedmont Community College, Cal State LA, and Youngstown State, were intended to have a positive impact on the local community or region served by the institution. Some such gifts came from individuals and businesses with an economic stake in the community, while others appear to have included an emotional element as well. For example, it is notable that YSU was able to tap into community loyalty on the part of donors who had grown up there and subsequently relocated, whom the case study refers to as Youngstown "ex pats."

Most higher-education donors who seek to have social impact choose to do so *through* their own institutions, perhaps suggesting a blend of social commitment and institutional loyalty (Langley, 2016). That is illustrated by the $50 million commitment that Martha and Bruce Karsh made to their alma mater, to establish the Karsh Institute of Democracy at UVA. And by Austin McChord's $50 million gift to the Rochester Institute of Technology. He sought to impact research, technology, and students. He did so not at MIT, but at RIT, which he had attended. The examples suggest that many principal gifts may occur when institutional loyalty, institutional priorities, institutional capabilities, and donors' interests all align.

Some people question whether the format of a campaign is consistent with the reality that individuals' readiness to give often is dependent on their own circumstances, rather than the institution's timetable. Older donors will consider major gifts in connection with their retirement or estate planning, that is, when they have reached the dispositive phase of their lives. Younger donors may give when they sell a business or receive a bonus, the timing of which is, again, related to their own circumstances rather than the deadlines imposed by a campaign. Some might argue that trying to force philanthropy into the deadlines defined by a campaign may result in less eventual support than nurturing relationships over time, guiding donors to discern their interests and values, and asking for a gift when the time is right for them and a purpose of mutual interest has emerged.

But long campaigns do provide the opportunity to cultivate relationships with prospective donors and to track their readiness to give within the campaign period. UVA received a $50 million commitment well into its public phase and YSU's largest gift came near the campaign's closing date. Relationships with those donors had preceded the campaign, but matured during the multi-year campaign period. In addition, the inclusion of bequest intentions in campaign totals and recognition programs can accommodate, and perhaps encourage, donors' long-term planning.

Institutional Dynamics

Institutional circumstances and priorities change and some might question how priorities established at the beginning of a long campaign can remain relevant as the campaign progresses. New programs and units may emerge on campus. Deans and other campus leaders, including presidents, may depart and new ones arrive, bringing different agendas. Presidents played a central role in all of the cases discussed in this book, articulating their visions for their institutions and initiating the strategic planning on which campaign priorities were based. In some cases, there was a change in the presidency during the campaign, requiring adjustments in campaign planning.

Changing conditions also may alter the relative importance of endowment and annual giving or the priority attached to scholarships, technology, or research. One clear example is the increased emphasis that most institutions gave to providing direct support to students during the Covid-19 pandemic, a need to which donors also responded.

Campaigns have adapted to the dynamic nature of institutional leadership and circumstances by defining priorities under broad pillars. That provides the flexibility to adjust specific goals to reflect changing conditions as the campaign proceeds. And some proposed new approaches, discussed later in this chapter, may offer even greater flexibility to shape ongoing campaigns to address emerging needs.

Changing Definitions of Community

Finally, some might say, the campaign model, developed more than a century ago, simply does not reflect the society in which we live today. Traditional concepts about communities, on which proportionate giving, sequential fundraising, and other traditional campaign principles are based, no longer apply in our mobile, global, and socially networked society.

But some gifts still do appear to have been influenced by the giving of others. For example, donors responded to the Winiarski Challenge gift to St. John's College, significantly expanding the college's donor constituency. In addition, today's campaigns have evolved to be more than intensive fundraising efforts. They are integrated initiatives to acquire additional resources as well as build engagement and community. Falling alumni participation in annual giving reflects many variables, including perhaps a declining sense of community. A campaign may be among the strategies for building community and expanding the base of support. For example, "We Are LA" became not only the name of Cal State LA's campaign but also a rallying point for its alumni and friends.

In sum, a campaign may not be the best strategy for every institution at all times. But the benefits remain substantial and the model has been adapted to accommodate emerging realities. It will need to continue evolving in order to remain effective in the years ahead.

NEW DIRECTIONS

There are three trends in particular that may define the future of campaigns: perpetual fundraising, donors' emphasis on impact, and an integrated approach to advancement. And, although the long-term effects of the Covid-19 pandemic cannot be known at the time of this writing, some of the innovations that were undertaken in response to its emergence may represent lasting change.

Perpetual Fundraising

Intensive university fundraising is now perpetual and is likely to remain so. Chapter 1 of this book discussed findings of a 2018 study by the marketing consulting firm Ruffalo Noel Levitz (2018) that identified trends in campaigns at that time. One was that perpetual campaigns had become the norm.

It may be useful to make a distinction between the idea that college and university *fundraising* is perpetual and the concept of a perpetual *campaign*. Fundraising for major and principal gifts is no longer episodic, it is perpetual. And some institutions may engage in perpetual campaigns by the definition of counting all commitments from the end of the previous campaign in totals for a new campaign. However, others may choose to bring their campaigns to a clean end, perhaps with the conclusion of a presidency and the beginning of a new strategic planning process. Indeed, there are likely to be pressures to do so, with new leaders wanting a fresh start and some constituents, for example the board and the faculty, skeptical of crediting gifts toward campaign totals without some gap. The CASE Global Standards may not be followed in all instances, but they are widely known and some people may question the desirability of departing from them substantially in terms of campaign length and counting policies.

Of course, the distinction between perpetual and clean break may not be that meaningful as the gap between campaigns continues to narrow. All of the institutions discussed in this book anticipated another campaign in the future and expected that the interval between campaigns will not be long. Indeed, chief advancement officers who were interviewed in the context of an ongoing campaign were already thinking about that next campaign. Thus, even when the campaign is not perpetual, campaign planning seems to be so.

Some suggest that as university fundraising becomes perpetual, campaigns may come to be defined primarily as marketing and communications umbrellas that span certain periods of time and encompass a series of shorter-term fundraising initiatives focused on specific projects or causes. The latter were traditionally called "mini campaigns," but that may incorrectly imply that their goals are necessarily modest. Consultant Karin George (2021) suggests the alternative terminology of "serial" campaigns or "a string of pearls." This approach could provide the flexibility to adjust fundraising efforts to address emerging priorities and opportunities over the course of a longer campaign.

Mark Luellen (2021), vice president at the University of Virginia, observes that "[UVA] is in a perpetual fundraising mode now and going forward" and identifies the challenge of maintaining "momentum and excitement" throughout a campaign that continues for years or never ends. He suggests that may be achieved by introducing new priorities and projects periodically. Perhaps a comprehensive campaign that encompasses a series of component campaigns—something like the "string-of-pearls" approach—may help to maintain momentum and attract support from donors whose priorities align with those particular efforts. It also may offer a strategy for accommodating changing university priorities that emerge over the course of the campaign.

Impact and the Case for Support

As discussed previously, donor motivations are varied and complex, but the desire to have impact—defined in various ways—has become characteristic of many principal and major gifts, which comprise a disproportionate amount of campaign totals.

Advancement thought leader James Langley, former vice president at Georgetown University, suggests a model that offers variations on traditional campaign practices in order to better align with that reality—what he calls the "emerging comprehensive campaign." Addressing donors' interest in achieving impact, he suggests some principles for defining and communicating campaign goals, including:

- Define campaign goals in terms of societal impact, not just dollars and broad priorities.
- Meet the desire of donors for impact by designing the campaign to demonstrate impact within 1–5 years rather than over a longer term.
- Determine the transition from the quiet to the public phase with an emphasis on mission milestones rather than a particular dollar amount raised. (Adapted from Langley, 2016, pp. 92–93)

These are interesting ideas, especially when campaign priorities include programs or projects for which outcomes may be readily measured. But it can be challenging to measure impact on larger social problems, as many nonprofit organizations have learned.

For example, it is certainly possible to measure the number of students from low-income backgrounds who are admitted to a university and how many complete their degrees (although in the language of evaluation, those are inputs and outputs, not measures of impact). On the other hand, a new research institute devoted to the study of climate change or democratic governance likely will accomplish good, but it may be difficult to evaluate the institute's impact on a major global issue, at least within a short period of years. An element of trust may be required.

The identification of campaign priorities also reflects internal considerations, especially at large and complex universities. Many have individual schools and units with their own strengths, priorities, and constituencies. The latter often include important donors and members of the governing or foundation board. The give and take within the university may require continuing to define campaign priorities in terms of broad consensus themes.

What will be required in planning future campaigns is thoughtful attention to building the institution's *case for support*, that is, its rationale for giving. That is not a new term or a new idea, but its meaning has become more complex. A solid case may include the institution's impact on social causes, local communities, and students, but also aspirations of the institution itself and the traditions that the institution upholds.

What is clear is that colleges and universities will need to engage substantively with their constituencies and cultivate meaningful relationships with their donors, in order to understand their values and *also* foster their understanding of the institution's aspirations. As Langley (2016) suggests, the dialogue may need to be ongoing, rather than be undertaken only as part of a feasibility study at initiation of planning for a new campaign. Data analytics play an important and growing part in developing fundraising strategies. But there can be no substitute for building relationships and real mutual understanding.

Integrated Institutional Advancement

The integration of strategic planning; the campaign; and marketing, communications, and branding initiatives has become established practice. Interestingly, almost 50 years after founding of the Council for Advancement and Support of Education, the concept of institutional advancement as an integrated discipline is being realized in the context of today's comprehensive campaigns.

For example, at RIT the campaign pillars were revised in the planning stage to be consistent with the messages developed as part of a new institution-wide marketing campaign. Tulane engaged a marketing firm to refine its campaign name (Only the Audacious: The campaign for an ever bolder Tulane), designed to capture the mindset of the university and its community following recovery from a disaster. Cal State LA's campaign name, "We Are LA," connected the university to its community and helped ignite overall institutional pride.

The integration of strategic planning and campaign planning also has become the norm. All of the institutions discussed in this book engaged in strategic planning in some form before launching the campaign and fundraising goals reflected the institutional priorities derived from that process.

As discussed in chapter 1 of this book, institutional planning and campaign planning are iterative processes—data from each is likely to influence the other. But there will be a need to maintain clarity and some caution. Strategic planning needs to reflect input from various constituents—potential donors as well as faculty, staff, the governing board, academic leaders, and the broader alumni constituency. Fundraising may be donor-driven, but academic priorities must also be consistent with fundamental aspirations and values of the college or university.

Campaign priorities need to hit the sweet spot between the institution's needs and the interests of donors. The case of RIT provides an interesting example in this regard. Knowing that alumni who had graduated in an earlier era might not be especially responsive to RIT's new ambitions as a research institution, two successive presidents designed an innovative campaign. The goal was to enhance research, while also maintaining a student-friendly environment valued by alumni. The campaign was designed to provide incentives for private support that could leverage government and corporate grants for research-oriented initiatives. In other words, campaign strategy was shaped by an understanding of the donor constituency as well as the institution's own over-arching goals.

The key word in the term "institutional advancement" is "institutional." As colleges and universities respond to the interests of impact-oriented donors, it will be important to remain mindful of this point. In setting their academic directions, colleges and universities may sometimes need to be, like St. Johns College, at least a little bit "contrarian."

THE POST-COVID WORLD

The campaigns discussed in this book were all active during the pandemic that afflicted the world during 2020 and 2021. How the institutions responded to that crisis is a part of the story in every case. At the time of this writing, it is not yet possible to predict the extent to which innovations introduced during the pandemic may represent permanent change.

The pandemic accelerated some changes that already were underway, for example, electronic communications and the use of video-conferencing technology for meetings and donor visits. It seems likely that digital fundraising will continue to replace direct mail, that phone solicitation will continue to decline, and that at least some donor contacts and alumni events will continue to be conducted remotely. However, these changes primarily reflect new techniques, that is, they are new ways of doing things and affect how people interact. They do not necessarily represent new fundraising strategies. But the pandemic may turn out to have a lasting effect on educational models as well as donor inclinations.

In the spring of 2021, higher-education writer David Rosowsky observed that the important questions for higher-education philanthropy in the post-Covid environment are connected to broader questions about the future of higher education. He credits colleges and universities with having responded to the pandemic with a degree of resilience and creativity that some found surprising for such mainstream institutions. They adopted remote learning, reduced overhead, and increased their flexibility in accommodating to students' situations.

Will the future include those or additional innovations? Will university faculty and staff fully return to their offices and classrooms or will some continue to work remotely? Will students, particularly undergraduates, still value the on-campus experience or will they and their families be more focused on value?

Rosowsky (2021) suggests that the answers to such questions may require adjustments in institutional and fundraising priorities, asking "Will [campus] amenities give way to access and affordability as priorities for donors? Will focus on student satisfaction give way to student success? Will there be a shift from building construction to building the needed supports . . . [that] ensure the success of all students, from all cultures and backgrounds?" Will donors demonstrate "greater empathy and inclination to support students directly, in the form of scholarships, funds to participate in high-impact practices (e.g., study abroad, undergraduate research, internships and other experiential learning, student travel grants), and to support programs that focus on student success rather than the student experience?" (Rosowsky, 2021).

Importantly, as Rosowsky acknowledges, the impact of such trends is likely to be different across *institution types*. As the case studies in this book illustrate, higher-education institutions in the United States comprise a vast array. Some are by their nature important instruments for social mobility. Some are the largest enterprise in their communities or regions. Some are esteemed centers of research that advance human knowledge. Others are committed to defending traditional principles. Some may be positioned to serve as vehicles for impact-oriented donors to pursue broader causes. Others will need to raise money to meet their own needs, in order to grow, even survive.

THE FUTURE OF COMPREHENSIVE CAMPAIGNS

This book began with the premise that campaigns will continue to be part of higher-education fundraising in the future. It reaches its conclusion with that same perspective. Comprehensive campaigns are a strategy for advancing institutions—raising money, building a culture of philanthropy, increasing visibility, and shaping a brand. Comprehensive campaigns surely will evolve, but they are likely to remain a visible part of the higher-education landscape.

There is not any single formula that will be successful for all higher-education institutions or for all campaigns. The traditional campaign model developed over many decades will continue to provide a *baseline*, from which colleges and universities can innovate in order to succeed in an ever-changing environment.

REFERENCES

Brooks, Jessie. 2021. Interview with author, June 1, 2021.
Dial, Janet Schellhase. 2021. Interview with author, June 7, 2021.
George, Karin. 2021. Email to author, April 19, 2021.
Langley, James M. 2016. *Comprehensive Fundraising Campaigns: A Guide for Presidents and Boards*. Denver, CO: Academic Impressions.
Luellen, Mark M. 2021. Interview with author, January 28, 2021.
Rosowsky, David. 2021. "Re-Thinking Higher Ed Fundraising Post-Pandemic: Finding The New Sweet-Spot Between Institutional Need And Donor Interest." *Forbes*, March 9. https://www.forbes.com/sites/davidrosowsky/2021/03/09/re-thinking-higher-ed-fundraising-post-pandemic-finding-the-new-sweet-spot-between-institutional-need-and-donor-interest/?sh=1b4831e566ba (accessed July 6, 2021).
Ruffalo Noel Levitz. 2018. *Advancement Leaders Speak: The Future of Higher Education Fundraising Campaigns*. Cedar Rapids, Iowa: author.
St. John's College. 2021. Freeing Minds. Website. https://freeingminds.sjc.edu/ (accessed July 8, 2021).
Worth, Michael J., Sheela Pandey, Sanjay K. Pandey, and Suhail Qadummi. 2020. "Understanding Motivations of Mega-Gift Donors to Higher Education: A Qualitative Study." *Public Administration Review*, March/April, 80 (2), 281–293.

Further Reading

Council for Advancement and Support of Education (CASE). 2021. *CASE Global Reporting Standards*. Washington, DC: Author.
Langley, James M. 2016. *Comprehensive Fundraising Campaigns: A Guide for Presidents and Boards*. Denver, CO: Academic Impressions.
Lippincott, John and Tom Mitchell (eds.) 2021. *Fundraising Campaigns in Higher Education: A Practical Guide for Governing and Foundation Boards*. Washington, DC: Association of Governing Boards of Universities and Colleges.
Logan, William Rhodes. 2015. *The Factors That Influenced the Decision to Enter Into a $1 billion Fundraising Campaign by Two Public Higher Education Institutions*. Dissertation, University of Tennessee-Knoxville. https://trace.tennessee.edu/utk_graddiss/3347/
Ruffalo Noel Levitz. 2018. *Advancement Leaders Speak: The Future of Higher Education Fundraising Campaigns*. Cedar Rapids, Iowa: author.
Schroder, Fritz W. 2019. "The Art and Science of Comprehensive Campaigns." In *Advancing Higher Education: New Strategies for Fundraising, Philanthropy, and Engagement*, edited by Michael J. Worth and Matthew T. Lambert, 113–128. Lanham, MD: Rowman & Littlefield.
Sevilla, Ed. 2018. "Best Practices for Aligning University Brands with Fundraising Campaigns." *Journal of Brand Strategy*, 7 (1), Summer, 69–83.
Worth, Michael J. 2017. *Leading the Campaign: The President and Fundraising in Higher Education*. Lanham, MD: Rowman & Littlefield.

About the Author

Michael J. Worth is Professor of Nonprofit Management in the Trachtenberg School of Public Policy and Public Administration at the George Washington University, where he teaches graduate courses on nonprofit management, fundraising, and philanthropy. He is also Principal of Michael J. Worth & Associates, LLC, a consulting firm that provides management and fundraising advice to colleges and universities, healthcare institutions, and nonprofit organizations.

He served as Vice President for Development and Alumni Affairs at the George Washington University and previously as Director of Development at the University of Maryland. Earlier in his career, he was Director of Development at DeSales University and Assistant to the President at Wilkes University. At GW, he planned and directed two comprehensive campaigns.

In addition to articles in academic and professional journals, he has written or edited widely read books, including *Leading the Campaign* (2010, 2017) and *Fundraising: Principles and Practice* (2016). His textbook, *Nonprofit Management: Principles and Practice*, is widely adopted in undergraduate ad graduate courses and is currently in its sixth edition. With Matthew T. Lambert, he is co-editor of *Advancing Higher Education: New Strategies for Fundraising, Philanthropy, and Engagement* (2019).

He holds a B.A. from Wilkes University, an M.A. in economics from the American University, and a Ph.D. from the University of Maryland.

LinkedIn: https://www.linkedin.com/in/michael-worth-4186709/

Amazon: https://www.amazon.com/Michael-J.-Worth/e/B001JRZU1C%3Fref=dbs_a_mng_rwt_scns_share

www.ingramcontent.com/pod-product-compliance
Lightning Source LLC
Chambersburg PA
CBHW030140240426
43672CB00005B/210